CLEP

Western Civilization 2
2012

Condensed Summary and Test Prep Guide

By David C. Haus and Michael D. Haus

CLEP Western Civilization 2

Copyright ©2012
All Rights Reserved
Printed in the USA

ISBN:#   978-1611045987

Published by:

Feather Trail Press, LLC
P. O. Box 7
Cedar Lake, Michigan 48812

Table of Contents

Famous People 4
Nations and Other Geographic Places 32

Battles and Wars 46
Eras and Movements 53
Political Alliances, Documents, and Treaties 56
Political and Cultural Forces 65
Political, Philosophical, and Scientific Ideas 70
Revolutions and Social Reforms 78

Famous People

Adam Smith (1723-1790):
- Scotsman who launched a vigorous attack on mercantilism
- often called the Father of Modern Economics

Adolph Hitler (1889-1945):
- became chancellor of Germany in 1933
- central to the founding of Nazism, the start of World War II, and chief perpetrator of the Holocaust
- devoted his first weeks in power to transforming his chancellorship into a dictatorship
- forced political parties that opposed him to dissolve (by July 1933, the Nazis were declared to be the only legal political party in Germany)
- banned communists and socialists (the nationalists dissolved themselves)
- instituted a ministry of propaganda under Joseph Goebbels
- stripped the state governments of their powers and made Germany a strongly centralized state
- forbade intermarriage between Jews and non-Jews, calling it "racial pollution"
- formed the Gestapo, or secret state police, to tap wires, view private correspondence, and spy on citizens
- created concentration camps for the killing of enemies of the state
- justified the conquest of all territories through German racism
- greatly admired Karl Lueger (anti-Semitic mayor of Vienna and model for Nazism), stating that Lueger was the greatest leader of his time
- developed his doctrines of Nazism while growing up under the racial and social structure of the Hapsburg dynasty

Famous People

Alexander II, Tsar of Russia (1818-1881):
- announced in 1861 that personal serfdom would be abolished and all peasants would be able to buy land from their landlords
- legislated the Emancipation Manifesto (law that freed the serfs)
  - the law proposed 17 legislative acts
  - the State would advance the money to the landlords and would recover it from the peasants in 49 annual sums known as redemption payments
- was mortally wounded by assassins shortly after Russia's first constitution was signed when two bombs were thrown at his carriage

Alexander III, Tsar of Russia (1845-1894):
- rose to power at a critical point in Imperial Russian history
- began his reign in tragedy after the assassination of Alexander II
- was considered to be Russia's last true autocrat
- epitomized what a Russian Tsar was supposed to be
- embodied the fabled Russian bear
- at 6'4" was considered to be very tall
- was forceful, formidable, and fiercely patriotic
- refused to grant the constitution due to the assassination of his father
- tightened censorship of the press
- sent thousands of revolutionaries to Siberia
- saw the Industrial Revolution come to Russia, and capitalism become popular, during his reign
- was hopelessly out of touch with the emerging realities of a modern, industrialized Russia
- determined to strengthen autocratic rule
- was quoted as saying that he intended to have "full faith in the justice and strength of the autocracy" he had been trusted with
- was very conservative, quickly dismissing any liberal proposals that came across his desk
- should have adjusted his government to the changing realities of the 19th century, rather than clinging to autocratic rule
- failed to satisfy liberals and radicals who desired freedom of expression, a parliamentary democracy, and agricultural reforms such as those enjoyed in the U.S. and most European states
- disappointed peasants with his agricultural reforms

- many peasants spent 20 years working to obtain their lands and were forced to pay much more than the land was worth

Arthur Balfour (1838-1930)
- British statesman who maintained a position of power in the British Conservative Party for 50 years
- served as British prime minister from 1902 to 1905 and foreign secretary from 1916 to 1919
- best remembered for his World War I statement (the Balfour Declaration) expressing official British approval of Zionism
- was derided by Winston Churchill, who stated that "If you wanted nothing done, Arthur Balfour was the best man for the task. There was no equal to him."

Benjamin Disraeli (1804-1881)
- considered to be Britain's first Jewish Prime Minister
- was actually a practicing Anglican despite his Jewish roots
- championed increasing democratism, social reform, and full emancipation of Jews
- remains controversial to this day, seen by some as central to a Jewish conspiracy to control the finances and political institutions of the world

Benjamin Franklin (1706-1790):
- open thinker, inventor, and American diplomat to France
- the embodiment of the Enlightenment in the eyes of the French
- showed that electricity and lightning were really the same
- the only American of the colonial period to earn a European reputation as a natural philosopher
- best remembered in the United States as a patriot and diplomat

Benito Mussolini (1883-1945):
- began his rise to power in Italy in 1918
- founded Fascism and gradually created a totalitarian state—in which he was the undisputed ruler
- obtained dictatorial powers, which were to last until the end of 1923, about a month after coming into office
- created a Fascist militia of 200,000 which garnered loyalty from his army

- coined the term totalitarianism
- summarized the totalitarian system where an all-powerful state regulated all aspects of life with his powerful quote: "everything in the state, nothing outside the state, and nothing against the state"
- ruled that emigration was a crime
- implemented a pro-birth policy that rewarded prolific Italian parents
    - saw this policy as the way to develop a larger army, together with stronger allegiance toward himself

Blaise Pascal (1623-1662):
- famous French mathematical genius and philosopher of the 17th century
- invented the barometer
- proved that air pressure diminishes with altitude
- known for his quote, "it is incomprehensible that God should exist, and it is incomprehensible that He should not exist"
- abandoned his scientific work late in life, devoting himself to philosophy and theology

Calvin Coolidge (1872-1933):
- U. S. president during the Stock Market Crash of 1929
- rose to national prominence when he used the militia to end the Boston police strike in 1919
- was nominated as Republican candidate for the vice presidency in 1920 and elected as V.P. to Warren G. Harding
- became President after Harding's death

Camillo Benso, Count of Cavour (1810-1861):
- great leader and leading figure in the movement toward Italian unification
- used the weapon of diplomacy to expel Austria, thereby unifying Italy

Catherine the Great, Empress of Russia (1729-1796):
- the most renowned and the longest-ruling female leader of Russia
- favored her grandson Alexander I as successor, rather than her son Paul (Paul did succeed her and rule before Alexander I took the throne, but only for five years before he was assassinated)
- was considered to be an enlightened despot
- under her rule, Russia became known as a great power in Europe

Charles I of Austria (1887-1922):
- also known as Charles IV of Hungary
- last ruler of the Austro-Hungarian empire

Charles Darwin (1809-1882):
- English naturalist
- chief proponent of the theory of evolution
- author of the book 'Origin of the Species'

Charles Dickens (1812-1870):
- considered to be the greatest novelist of the Victorian period
- created some of the world's most memorable fictional characters (Scrooge, Tiny Tim, etc.)
- was a compassionate observer of the development of industrial England
- argued against the teachings of utilitarians and the laissez-faire liberals

Charles Fourier (1772-1837):
- influential French philosopher and thinker
- credited with coining the word "feminism"
- best remembered for his writings on a new world order based on unity of action and harmonious collaboration

Copernicus (1473-1543):
- Polish astronomer who advanced the heliocentric theory in the sixteenth century
    - heliocentrism is the astronomical model in which the Earth and planets revolve around a stationary Sun at the center of the universe
    - before Copernicus it was commonly believed that the sun moved around the earth

Edmund Burke (1729-1797):
- philosophical founder of Conservatism
- wrote a famous book called "Reflections on the Revolution in France" in 1790
- believed that society was a contract, nothing more than a partnership agreement between a government and its citizens, and as such is by nature a temporary arrangement which can be dissolved

Eli Whitney (1765-1825):
- American inventor best known for inventing the cotton gin (1793)
    - an engine that separated the fibers of raw cotton from the seeds
    - one of the key inventions of the Industrial Revolution
    - enabled a single slave to do what had previously required the hand labor of 50 slaves
    - vastly influenced the economy of the Antebellum South

Ferdinand II (1578-1637):
- Hapsburg's emperor from 1619 to 1637
- Holy Roman emperor and king of Bohemia as well as Hungary
- successor to the Holy Roman emperor Matthias
- played a major role in the Thirty Years war

Flora Tristan (1803-1844):
- French social writer and activist
- one of the founders of modern feminism

Francis Ferdinand (1863-1914):
- Archduke of Austria whose assassination in Sarajevo triggered events leading to World War I
- married to Sophie Chotek, who was assassinated with him

Frederick the Great (1712-1786):
- regarded as one of the most enlightened monarchs of his time
- initiated several reforms including the elimination of torture, limited freedom of the press, freedom of speech and complete religious toleration
- declined to change the system of serfdom because of his dependence on nobility, although serfdom was condemned by enlightened thinkers
- reversed his father's policy of allowing commoners upward mobility in the civil service
    - limited the top offices to nobles

Frederick II the Great (1740-1786):
- the ruler most in tune with the beliefs of the Enlightenment
- had the nickname "Old Fritz"

Frederick William (1620-1688):
- known as the Great Elector, or the Elector of Brandenburg
- first in a line of Hohenzollern rulers
- won recognition from Poland as the full sovereign of Prussia
- held office from 1640 until his death in 1688
- affirmed the Hohenzollern pattern of militarized absolutism
    - a policy in which he was assisted by a Lutheran state church and an educational tradition that taught the virtues of obedience and discipline
    - Absolutism is rule by a single person—one with absolute authority

Francis Bacon (1561-1626):
- lawyer and lord chancellor in 17th century England
- proponent of the collection and observation of data
- encouraged scientists to acquire knowledge based on inductive principles
- proposed that scientists must believe all things possible until all things could be tested (in his book *Novum Organum*)
- invented the Scientific Method
    - the development of knowledge through organized experiments and thorough, systematic observations

Franklin Delano Roosevelt (1882-1945):
- 32nd president of the United States
- also known as FDR
- central figure in world events during the mid-20th century
- led the U.S. during a time of worldwide economic depression and World War II
- the only American president elected to more than two terms
- suffered from polio

Galileo (1564-1642):
- great Italian astronomer, mathematician, and physicist
- invented the telescope, which greatly enlarged humanity's vision and conception of the universe
- laid the foundation for modern experimental science by persistently investigating natural laws
- gave a mathematical formulation to many physical laws
- wrote "I hold the sun to be situated motionless in the center of the revolution of the celestial bodies, while the earth rotates on its axis and revolves about the sun"
- argued that the testimony of biblical passages should not take precedence over observable facts
    - was called before the Inquisition in Rome in 1633 and forced to recant his "heresies"
- fueled the ideas of the Scientific Revolution with his writings, which spread throughout Europe

CLEP Western Civilization 2

George C. Marshall (1880-1959):
- American military leader and general during the World War II era
- noted as the "organizer of victory" by Winston Churchill
- served as the United States Army Chief of Staff and chief military adviser to President Roosevelt during the war
  - was instrumental in developing the Marshall Plan (large-scale American program of economic aid to European countries after World War II designed to prevent the spread of Soviet communism)
- won a Nobel Prize for the Marshall Plan in 1953

George Eugene Haussmann (1809-1891):
- commissioned by Napoleon III to modernize Paris
- largely responsible for the beauty of modern Paris
- widened streets, laid out boulevards and parks, built sewers, barracks, and bridges

Guiseppe Garibaldi (1807-1882):
- an important figure in the cause of Italian Liberation
- led the volunteer "Red Shirt" army of 1,067 men who invaded Sicily before turning their attention to conquering the North of Italy
- won support wherever he went through natural charisma
- achieved remarkable victories on the battlefield, even when greatly outnumbered, through personal courage and clever military tactics

Giuseppe Mazzini (1805-18720:
- Italian politician, journalist, and activist who helped inspire Italian Nationalism
- established the secret society known as Young Italy, which was devoted to uniting Italy
- nicknamed "The Beating Heart of Italy"

Famous People

Harry Truman (1884-1972):
- 33rd president of the United States
- succeeded President Franklin Roosevelt after Roosevelt died in office
- is remembering for his upset presidential victory in 1948 over Thomas Dewey, authorizing the dropping of the atomic bomb, and the Fair Deal economic plan

Heinrich Heine (1797-1856):
- poet, critic, and a satirist of the government in Germany
- not officially a member of the Young Germans, thought allied with them in many beliefs and ideals
- voluntarily exiled to Paris in 1831 after facing difficulty in Germany
- lived in Paris for the rest of his life

Isaac Newton (1642-1747):
- knighted by Queen Anne and became known as "Sir Isaac Newton"
- invented Calculus
    - the Latin meaning of the word calculus is a small counting stone.
- formulated the concept of gravity and the three Laws of Motion, which were one of his greatest achievements and are still in use today

Herbert Hoover (1874-1964):
- 31st president of the United States
- due to his belief in keeping the government out of economic troubles, will always be blamed for the Great Depression
- developed the plan of "meatless Mondays, wheatless Wednesdays" while heading up the USDA for then-president Woodrow Wilson

Jacques Brissot (1754-1793):
- leading member of the Girondist movement during the French
- opposed the execution of Louis XVI, favoring a house arrest instead
- met his own end on the guillotine, partly due to his stance regarding Louis XVI

James Watt (1736-1819):
- invented the first steam engine in 1769
    - the steam engine was an important contribution to the industrial revolution
- improved on Thomas Newcomen's 1760's steam engine design
- made the machine much more versatile and efficient by featuring a rotary engine which could turn a shaft and drive machinery

Jean-Baptiste Colbert (1619-1683):
- great French practitioner of mercantilism
- controller general early in the personal reign of Louis XIV
- served as the French minister of Finance from 1665 to 1683

Jean-Jacques Rousseau (1712-1778):
- Swiss-French philosopher, author, political theorist, and composer
- known as the "Father of Romanticism"
- proposed revisions against strict, disciplined education
- became famous for creating the Social Contract
    - a progressive work that helped inspire political reforms or revolutions in Europe (especially France)
    - written in an attempt to reconcile the liberty of the individual with the institution of the government
- asserted that a perfect society would be controlled by the "general will" of its citizens
- did not suggest a method for the implementation of the perfect society

Jean-Paul Marat (1743-1793):
- physician, political theorist, and scientist
- best known for his career in France as a radical journalist and politician during the French Revolution
- loudly denounced many members of the Girondin political party as traitors
- deputies countered by calling for the impeachment of Marat

Jean-Paul Sartre (1905-1980):
- the most important philosopher of Existentialism (which was founded by Soren Kierkegaard)
- made the term Existentialism popular by using it for his own philosophy

Jeremy Bentham (1738-1842):
- an eccentric philosopher and patron of the classical economists
- devised dozens of schemes to improve the human race
- coined new words such as codify, minimize, and international
    - founded his social teachings on utilitarianism (the concept of utility), which teaches that the goal of action should be to achieve the greatest good for the greatest number

John Law (1671-1729):
- Scottish economist, gambler, banker, murderer, royal advisor, exile, rake and adventurer
- served the economic director of France
- vastly impacted France's economy through his economic plan

John Locke (1632-1704):
- English philosopher educated at Oxford
- father of liberalism
- founder of British empiricism
- exerted a profound and incalculable influence on philosophy and political theory
- penned *An Essay Concerning Human Understanding*, where he:
    - objected to the divine or absolute right of monarchies
    - denied the existence of innate ideas and tendencies that people are born with
    - developed his blank slate theory (known as Tabula Rasa)
- developed the underlying tenets of the social contract theory, which argues that individuals have consented to surrender some of their freedoms and submit to the authority of a ruler in exchange for protection of their natural rights
- proposed that:
    - the state exists to preserve the natural rights of its citizens
    - all people by nature are free

- - o people submitted passively to government because they found it convenient to do so, not because they acknowledged any divine right on the part of the monarchy
  - o "by nature, all men are free, equal, and independent" (direct quote)
- defended England's "Glorious Revolution"
- was followed by Rationalists

John Stuart Mill (1806-1873):
- expressed his humane liberalism in his writings "Utilitarianism", "The Subjection of Women", and "On Liberty" (make a book of these three)
- published and revised his books repeatedly, always moving away each time from the "dismal science" of Malthus and Ricardo
  - o "dismal science" is a derogatory alternative name for economics devised by the Victorian historian Thomas Carlyle in the 19th century
- was associated with liberalism
- was good friends with Jeremy Bentham
- an early supporter of women's rights
- "On Subjection of Women" was the name of his famous book
- believed that with equal education, women could accomplish as much as men
- one of the first to support giving women the right to vote

Joseph II (1741-1790):
- emperor of Austria
- considered the most truly enlightened of the Enlightened Despots of Europe
- worked hard to increase the welfare of his country
- abolished serfdom
- passed the Toleration Patent, which declared all Lutheran, Greek Orthodox, and Calvinist churches could freely worship without official harassment
- eased oppression of Jews in his country

Joseph Stalin (1878-1953):
- broke the promise of free elections he made at Yalta
- refused to allow self-determination in what was clearly becoming a Soviet bloc in Eastern Europe
- stated that a freely elected government in any East European country would be anti-Soviet and therefore, could not be allowed
- had been a member of Russia's Bolshevik central committee since 1912
- entered the Soviet cabinet as "People's Commisar for Nationalities"
- began to emerge as a leader in the new regime after the Revolution of 1917
- desired to identify the Totalitarian rule of the Communist Party with stability and legitimacy
- basically repudiated the basic Marxist tenet of the "withering away" of the state
- glorified the state rather than have it "wither away"

Karl Lueger (1844-1910):
- the most famous Christian Socialist leader and the mayor of Vienna
- the idol of lower middle classes
- sponsored public ownership of city utilities, parks, playgrounds, free milk for school children, and other welfare services
- hailed by Adolph Hitler as the greatest leader of his time

Khedive (1769-1849):
- ruler of Egypt from 1867 to 1914
- governed as a viceroy of the sultan of Turkey
- also known as Muhammad Ali of Egypt

Lord Durham (1792-1840):
- British statesman and colonial administrator who served as High Commissioner for North America
- also known as "Radical Jack"
- helped merger upper and lower Canada, and assisted in installing a democratic government

Louis XIV (1638-1715):
- also known as Louis the Great or the Sun King
- believed himself to be a representative of God on earth
    - his rule was a typical divine right monarchy
    - he ruled for 72 years, the longest reign in European history
    - his rule typified the period of absolute monarch in the second half of the 17th century, during which the kings ruled without the restraint of representative institutions
- revoked the Edict of Nantes in 1685, which had guaranteed the following rights to the Huguenots as well as other religious sects:
    - full liberty of conscience and private worship
    - liberty of public worship wherever it had previously been granted
    - full civil rights including the right to hold public office
    - royal subsidies for Protestant schools special courts, composed of Roman Catholic and Protestant judges, to judge cases involving Protestants
- used etiquette and ceremony at the court of Versailles as a way of controlling nobles and enhancing his personal authority
- cut the high nobility and princes off from their influence in the countryside by keeping them involved in the myriad activities that made up daily life at Versailles
- developed an elaborate ritual centered around his own person, where every royal action was accompanied by great ceremony and proud aristocrats contended for the honor of emptying the king's chamber pot or handing him his shirt
- presided over a French judicial and legal system that needed entire reform (especially the two legal systems)
    - the courts needed a thorough overhaul to make them swift, fair, and inexpensive
- saw his ambitious military plans for French expansion come to an end with the Treaty of Utrecht

Famous People

Louis XV (1710-1774):
- enjoyed a favorable reputation at the beginning of his reign
- and earned the epithet "the Beloved" during that time
- the debauchery of his court, his ill-advised financial policies, and unpopular military decisions made him one of the most unpopular kings in the history of France
- was uninterested in politics and largely influenced by his chief mistress, Madame de Pompadour
- ultimately damaged the power of France, weakened the treasury, discredited the absolute monarchy, and helped trigger the French Revolution (which broke out 15 years after his death)

Louis XVI (1754-1793):
- ruled France up until the time of the French Revolution, when he died by the guillotine
- was married to Marie Antoinnette, who also died by the guillotine
- was well aware of the growing discontent of the French population against the absolute monarchy
- attempted to reform France in accordance with Enlightenment ideals (abolition of torture and serfdom, religious tolerance), however, his reforms stumbled due to hostility from the nobles
- was declared guilty of treason and sentenced to die on the guillotine after 100 hours of continuous voting by Robespierre and the "Republic of Virtue"
- executed on January 21, 1793
- the only king of France ever to be executed

Louis Blanc (1811-1882):
- French socialist and Politian who favored reforms and sought to help the urban poor
- greatly influenced the development of socialism in France
- was a great orator

Madame Dudevant (1804-1876):
- famous French novelist and memoirist who used the pen name George Sand

Marie Antoinette (1755-1793):
- Hapsburg empress and queen to the French monarch Louis XVI
- reminded French patriots of the ill-fated alliance with Austria during the Seven Years War
- was rumored to have said "Let them eat cake" upon hearing that her subjects had no bread to eat (the story was spread in the lively gossip papers of Paris)
- died by the guillotine nine months after the execution of her husband

Marquis de Condorcet (1743-1794):
- French philosopher, mathematician, and political scientists
- wrote the book "The Progress of the Human Mind"
- wrote about the optimistic implications of the world-machine belief, also known as the clockwork universe theory, which compares the universe to a mechanical clock wound up by a supreme being or initiated by the Big Bang
    - the book was written while de Condorcet was hiding from political persecution during the French Revolution's Reign of Terror
- was captured while attempting to flee Paris, and died a mysterious death in prison two days later
    - may have drunk poison provided to him by a friend, or been considered too popular to die by the guillotine

Maximilien Robespierre (1758-1794):
- a young lawyer and a political extremist who demanded a Republic of Virtue
    - The Republic of Virtue was a period in French history from 1791 to 1794
- key figure during the French Revolution
- together with the "Republic of Virtue," ruled France during the French Revolution,
- radical leader of the Jacobins, who ascended to power with the establishment of the Revolutionary dictatorship in 1793, and were:
    - one of the most famous political groups of the French Revolution
    - instruments of the Reign of Terror

- o nicknamed the Montagnards (meaning "Mountain") because they took benches high in the back of the assembly during the hall at a National Convention held during the French Revolution)

Mikhail Gorbachav (1931—) :
- Soviet statesman and last head of the Soviet Union before its dissolution in 1991
- initiated a series of political, economic and social reforms called perestroika, or restructuring, during the 1980s
- originally planned only to restructure the Soviet economy
- soon learned that the Soviet economy was closely linked to the nation's political and social systems
- instituted a policy of glasnost (openness), which encouraged Soviet citizens to openly discuss the strengths and weaknesses of their country
  - o Glasnost resulted in a freer political and cultural life in which criticism of the party and the state were permitted
  - o even TV broadcasts which depicted the quagmire in Afghanistan were allowed

Montesquieu, or Charles-Louis de Secondat (1689-1755):
- French lawyer, baron, and political thinker
- set out to analyze England's political and economic virtues as compared to those of France
- found a superior concept of checks and balances in English government
- divided the society of France into three classes, the monarchy, the aristocracy, and the commons

Nicholas I of Russia (1825-1855):
- came to the throne amid the disorders of the Decembrist Revolution
- known as a reactionary and autocratic leader
- presided over the investigation of the revolutionaries and prescribed their punishment
- lived in fear of future revolution
- confidently expected the collapse of the Ottoman Empire
- wished to protect the Orthodox subjects of the sultan

- had important economic interests at stake in the wheat-producing areas of the south

Napoleon Bonaparte (1769-1821):
- French military and political leader who rose to prominence during the latter stages of the French Revolution
- slowly increased his authority over time
- he persuaded French legislators to drop the ten year limit on his term to office and make him the first consul for life in 1802
- prompted the French Senate to declare that "the government of the republic is entrusted to an emperor" in 1804
- crowned as French emperor in a magnificent coronation ceremony at Notre Dame in Paris on December 2, 1804
- enacted a series of laws known as the "Code of Napoleon"
- declared all men equal before the law without regard to rank or wealth
- revived some of the glamor of the Old Regime, but not its glaring inequalities
- promoted principles of the French Revolution, such as:
    - religious tolerance
    - equality before the law
    - appointment to political office based on merit rather than birth
    - protection of private property
    - the elimination of serfdom
- restored the rights of fathers over their families
- was not as favorable to the rights of women
    - women lost some of their rights under Napoleon
    - during Napoleon's reign it became more difficult for women to obtain a divorce
- suffered naval defeat at the hands of the British at Trafalgar in October, 1805
    - the British fleet was led by their naval hero, Lord Admiral Nelson
    - England's resounding victory confirmed British naval supremacy
    - France was allied with Spain at the Battle of Trafalgar
- initiated the Continental System (also known as the Continental Blockade) in retaliation to the naval defeat at Trafalgar, which:

- was a "commercial war" instituted in 1806 and intended to starve Britain into submission by closing European markets to England
    - featured a Europe-wide boycott of British goods, which were barred from European ports and were to be seized in all French and allied territories
    - backfired when British merchants began smuggling goods into continental Europe, where Napoleon's land-based custom's officers could not stop them
    - served as a prime example of Napoleon's imperialism
        - attempted to regulate the economy of the entire continent through a self-blockade that tied political, military, and economic goals into a single European policy
        - was designed to make France the center of a Grand Empire
- issued the Berlin Decree in 1806, which:
    - forbade all trade with the British Isles
    - ordered the arrest of all Britons in France and the confiscation of their property
- was resisted by the British, who were the first to resist him successfully—at Trafalgar and on the economic battlefields of the Continental System
- reached the pinnacle of his military career in 1807, when he:
    - met with Czar Alexander I of Russia on a raft in Tilsit (between East Prussia and Russia)
    - drew up a treaty with the Czar dividing Europe between them
    - Napoleon promised to share the spoils of the Ottoman Empire with Russia if France was able to defeat it, in return for:
        - the cease of trade between England and Russia
        - an agreement for Russia to side with France against England
- turned on Spain, which had formerly been his ally, attacking in 1807
- invaded Russia in 1812
    - the war resulted in the death of nearly 300,000 French troops and the capture of an additional 200,000
    - most died from cold and starvation during the Great Retreat

- was opposed by a coalition of almost every nation in Europe by the year 1813
  - Napoleonic imperialism had aroused a nationalistic reaction among disunited Germans, whose intellectuals launched a campaign to check the great influence that the French language and culture had gained over their divided lands
- was defeated by the allied armies of Austria, Prussia, and Russia in 1813 and 1814
  - allied forces captured Paris and exiled Napoleon to the Island of Elba
- escaped from the island of Elba in and returned to France in 1815
- formed an army of loyal veterans and fought the Battle of Waterloo in Belgium in 1815, which was:
  - Napoleon's last battle, ending his rule as Emperor of France
  - a decisive victory for the British and Prussians who had combined forces under the command of the Duke of Wellington
- was free from exile for only 100 days
- was re-exiled, this time to the distant island of St. Helena, where he spent the remaining six years of his life, dying in 1821

Nicholas II of Russia (1868-1918):
- presided over a period when Russia went from being one of the foremost great powers of the world to economic and military collapse
- was nicknamed Bloody Nicholas because of the Khodynka Tragedy, Bloody Sunday, the anti-Semitic programs, his execution of political opponents, and pursuit of military campaigns on a hitherto unprecedented scale
- commanded the Russian army during World War I
- left Russia under the rule of his wife (who was advised by Rasputin) while he was off to war
- abdicated after the revolution of 1917
- was killed, together with his wife, children, and some close associates, by the Bolsheviks in 1918

Oliver Cromwell (1599-1658):

- English political and military leader
- nicknamed "Old Ironsides"
- was a signatory on the death warrant of King Charles I
- ruled as "Lord Protector" of England for a short time
- one of the most controversial figures in the history of the British Isles
    - seen by some as a dictator and by others as a promoter of democracy
    - his measures against Catholics in Scotland and Ireland were near-genocidal

Otto von Bismarck (1815-1898):
- Prime Minister of Germany and powerful German leader during the 1860s
- known as the Founder of the German Empire
- strengthened German unity and power by calling on the nationalistic tendencies of the German people
- served as Germany's first Chancellor from 1871 to 1890
- devoted himself to unifying the German states
- is remembered for his greatest achievements, which were:
    - administrative reforms
    - developing a common currency
    - a central bank
    - a single code of commercial and civil law for Germany
- campaigned against the Catholic Center Party to destroy Catholicism in Germany, by implementing a policy known as Kulturkampf, under which a number of anti-Catholic laws were passed, including:
    - restrictions on Catholic worship and education
    - limitations on movement of the clergy
    - laws dissolving religious orders
- created a culture of militarism that:
    - glorified the military
    - promoted military domination and the buildup of arms
    - resulted in a series of wars against the Austrians and the French
- united Germany through his policy of Real Politik
- goaded France into declaring war on Prussia in 1870 by publishing a French telegram which he edited to make it appear insulting to the French

- the southern German states joined Prussia and the French were quickly defeated
- in the resulting treaty, France agreed to pay an indemnity of 5 billion francs and surrender the provinces of Alsace and Lorraine to Germany
- this humiliation angered the French and left them seeking revenge

Peter the Great (1672-1725):
- ruled Russia from 1672 until his death in 1725
- oversaw Russia's rise as a major power under his reign
- shared the throne with his brother Ivan until Ivan's death in 1696
- launched a program of forced westernization after visiting the West in 1698:
    - his motive was to make Russia a great military power, which he believed could only be accomplished through westernization
    - tried to force the country to adopt European appearance and other aspects of Western culture
- moved the capital of Russia from Moscow to a new city he had built—St. Petersburg
- spent most of his 43-year year reign at war
    - Russia was only at peace for one year during his entire reign
- replaced the former taxation system, which taxed only land and households, with a tax on everyone, including serfs and paupers
    - the tax, which was levied on every male head, was known as the "Soul Tax
- curbed the power of the nobles, basing privileges on service rather than birth
    - introduced the Table of Ranks in 1722, which:
        - promoted people based on loyalty to the tsar rather than birth or seniority
        - consisted of 14 ranks
        - required individuals to qualify for promotion from one rank to another
            - those in ranks 1-5 received personalized attention from the Emperor
- angered the lower classes of Russia, including the Cossacks, peasants, village priests, and laborers, who:

- - suffered an ever increasing tax burden because of his endless wars
    - were all hostile to his reforms
    - rose up against him in "peasant uprisings," which were punished with extreme brutality
    - peasant uprisings generally involved an alliance of the peasants with the Cossacks (militaristic communities of various ethnicities that occurred in Eastern Europe)
- alienated the clergy with his insulting behavior toward the Church
- benefited upper class women through his social reforms
    - women were given the right to choose who they married
    - it was made acceptable for men and women to mix socially

Philip V of Spain (1683-1746):
- longest reigning monarch in Spanish history (more than 45 years)
- grandson of Louis XIV of France
- first member of the House of Bourbon to rule Spain

Rasputin (1869-1916):
- advisor to the wife of Czar Nicholas II during World War I
- gained so much influence in the imperial family that he was rumored among Russians to be the ruler
- may have helped to discredit the Czarist government, leading to the fall of the Romanov dynasty
- could have been a scapegoat, rather than the cause, of the fall of imperialism

Rembrandt (1606-1669):
- Dutch painter
- created dozens of realistic portraits of Burghers of his day (a Burger is a middle class citizen that lives in a city)
- focused on painting religious scenes later in his life
- recognized as the greatest Protestant painter of the seventeenth century
- died bankrupt

René Descartes (1596-1650):
- French philosopher, mathematician, and scientist
- the most articulate spokesman for rationalism and materialism
- spoke of his mistrust of authority, both theological and intellectual
- significantly influenced the transition from medieval science and philosophy to the modern era through his methodology

Richard Wagner (1813-1833):
- created a series of four operas called "The Ring of Nibelung"
- inspired by the great German epic myth, Nibelungenlied
- gave new significance to old Teutonic myths through his operas, since he used them to express his aspirations for a stronger national identity for Germany

Robert Owen (1771-1858):
- cotton magnate, Utopian socialist and a leader of the union movement of the early 1800s
- believed in fostering cooperation through the creation of voluntary associations
- remembered for transforming a filthy Scottish factory town (Lanark) into a thriving, healthy community

Salvador Dali (1904-1989):
- identified with the artistic movement known as Surrealism
  - during wartime, Surrealism was a key artistic movement in which disturbing images were used to portray fantasies, dreams and nightmares
  - Surrealist art emphasizes the irrational
- Dali's paintings were characterized by recognizable objects displayed out of context

Sigmund Freud (1856-1939):
- Austrian psychiatrist
- known as the "Father of Psychoanalysis"
- influenced the understanding of human relationships, and, as a result, vastly impacted political and social theory

Soren Kierkegaard (1813-1855):
- Danish philosopher, theologian, and religious author
- widely considered to be the first existentialist philosopher

Thomas Jefferson (1743-1826):
- American founding father
- chief author of the Declaration of Independence
- 3rd President of the United States
- marked the highpoint of The Age of Reason when he said that "every man had two homelands; his own and France"

Thomas Malthus (1766-1834):
- famous 19th century classical economist
- the first professional economist
- hired by the East India Company to teach its employees at a training school in England
- initially educated to be a minister
- published "The Principle of Population" in 1798
    o predicted a world population explosion and warning that the human species would breed itself into starvation
    o warned that while the population increased at a geometric rate, the food supply increased much more slowly and would soon be insufficient to feed the hungry masses
- disapproved of England's Poor Laws, a modest welfare system which was locally administered
- believed a welfare system would inevitably increase population without increasing food production, leading to mass starvation
- David Ricardo, also a classical economist, was a famous peer of Malthus, also a classical economist

Thomas Newcomen (1664-1729):
- created the first steam engine in 1712
    o it was used to pump water out of flooded mine shafts

Vladimer Lenin (1870-1924):
- Russian communist revolutionary, politician and political theorist
- served as the Premier of the Soviet Union from 1922 to 1924
- the most important of the Bolsheviks

- enabled the Bolsheviks to emerge as a political threat through his transformation and adaptation of Marxist doctrine
- possessed supreme tactical skill and boldness, which served him well in bringing the Bolsheviks (who were a minority) to power during the Revolution of 1917
- foresaw the course of the Revolution and, as a result, pressed the Bolshevik party's central committee to organize an armed insurrection and seize power
- With the aid of fellow Bolshevik leader Trotsky:
    - created a Bolshevist constitution
    - established a dictatorship of the proletariat
    - defended the dictatorship by arguing that no oppressed class had ever come to power without passing through a dictatorship first
- applied socialism on a national scale
- abolished private property ownership
- enabled government takeover of manufacturing and production

Voltaire (1694-1778):
- French essayist and philosopher who wrote under the pen name François-Marie Arouet
- most famous philosopher of the Enlightenment
- most remembered for his criticism of organized religion and outspoken support for religious toleration
- wrote *Candide*, a tale that ridiculed optimists and *The Ignorant Philosopher*
    - both criticized religion and religious intolerance

Warren Harding (1865-1923):
- 23rd President of the United States
- influential and self-made newspaper publisher
- died suddenly of unknown causes while in office
- succeeded by President Calvin Coolidge

Famous People

William Pitt the Elder (1708-1778):
- known as "The Great Commoner"
- strengthened Britain's Anglo-Prussian alliance through the replacement of inefficient generals
- successfully transformed naval and colonial campaigns
- namesake for several American cities and towns, including Pittsburgh, PA

Winston Churchill (1864-1975):
- British politician who led England during World War II
- noted statesman and orator
- one of the greatest wartime leaders of the 20th century

Woodrow Wilson (1856-1924):
- 28th President of the United States
- campaigned in the 1916 presidential election on a pledge to keep the U.S. out of the war if possible
- controlled the American military during World War I
- became disabled during his term of office, a fact which was hidden from the vice president and the public until after his death

Nations and Other Geographic Places

Austria:
- originally part of the German empire
- became one of the great powers of Europe during the 17th and 18th centuries
- was proclaimed as the Austrian Empire in 1804, in response to the coronation of Napoleon as Emperor of France
- was re-formed into the dual monarchy of Austria-Hungary in 1867 through a unique compromise
- had Vienna as its largest city, as well as its social, political, and cultural center
  - much of Vienna's widely hailed charm was created by the Jewish minority, which:
    - was often forced to enter the trades (as opposed to the professions) due to anti-Semitism
    - cultivated Austrian music, cafes, newspapers, medicine, and science.
  - was home to the most famous Christian Socialist leader, Karl Lueger, who served as mayor of Vienna

Austria-Hungary:
- formation in 1867 was motivated by a desire for:
  - protection of the Hapsburg dynasty
  - a shared emperor who would always be Catholic and a legitimate Hapsburg
- the Austrian constitution of 1867 provided that all nationalities should enjoy equal rights and guaranteed that each could use its own language and education, administration, and public life
  - the theory sounded wonderful
  - in practice neither the Austrians nor the Hungarians respected the statutes
  - the minorities suffered inconsistently applied discrimination and persecution
- after the dual monarchy developed, the Czechs felt entitled to a compromise which would give them a voice in the government
  - the Czechs hoped to add a third power into the mix, thereby ensuring their own rights through representation

- the attempted union of the two countries led to chronic instability, as they never merged fully
- liberals in Austria-Hungary:
    - fought clerical conservatives over religious issues
    - forced through bills legalizing civil marriages, secularized schools, and taxes on church property
    - were discredited by the financial crash of 1873, during which it was revealed that some of them had accepted bribes
- the middle class in Austria was small:
    - after the financial crash of 1873, the working class favored socialism
    - among the bourgeoisie (wealthier classes) were many Jews, who generally could not be nobles, bureaucrats, or army officers
- Austrian nobles:
    - often owned great estates which they ran like independent rulers
    - took little interest in the nation's problems
- Austrian peasants:
    - held very small pieces of land, due to the large size of estates of the nobility
    - often had to seek supplementary employment on the property of nobles
- stresses of the Austria-Hungary social structure led to the formation of two important new political groups among the Austrians and Germans:
    - Pan-Germans, a radical group who:
        - opposed both the Hapsburg dynasty and the Catholic church
        - demanded that Austria become Protestant
        - agitated for political union with Germany
    - Christian Socialists (a major conservative political party from 1891-1934)
- was annexed and occupied by Nazi Germany during World War II

Balkans:
- one of several independent new nations on the Balkan Peninsula in southeastern Europe which had formerly been part of the Ottoman Empire

- included territory now held by Serbia, Croatia, Bulgaria, and Albania—among other countries
- the line between Roman Catholic Europe and Orthodox Greeks / Asian Muslims lay in the Balkans
- known as "The Powder Keg of Europe" prior to World War II because of longstanding religious and ethnic hatred

Bastille:
- a famous French prison
- stormed at the beginning of the French Revolution
- only released seven prisoners
- had an enormous symbolic significance
- the destruction of the Bastille signified the fall of the Old Regime
- as a result, July 14 became a great French holiday (similar to the American Fourth of July)
- at that time, more than 250,000 Parisians were united and under arms

Czechoslovakia:
- declared independence from the Austro-Hungarian empire in 1918, as the Czechs:
    - represented the minority nationality under the dual monarchy of Austria-Hungary
    - were substantial in population, and in the best position of the minorities within Austria-Hungary to exercise independence
    - had a high percentage of artisan skills
- was overrun by Nazi Germany during World War II
- lost its eastern portion, the Carpathian Ruthenia, to the Soviet Union in 1945
- peacefully split into Slovakia and the Czech Republic in 1993

Egypt:
- was strategically important to the colonial interests of England
    - overland travel through Egypt was the fastest way for the English to reach India
- the English fought Napoleon for control of Egypt in 1798
    - at first successful, they were later forced out of Egypt in 1805 and didn't return for 75 years

Nations and Other Geographic Places

- British interest in Egypt reawakened in 1869 with the opening of the Suez Canal
    - England gained a stronghold by controlling the French-built Suez Canal
    - the canal was considered England's lifeline to India
- in the years that followed, the British outmaneuvered the French and brought Egypt under Imperial British control
- Egypt was virtually subject to by England by World War I
    - still part of the Ottoman Empire
    - the khedive's government remained, but
    - a British resident was always at hand

England/Great Britain:
- England united with Scotland to become Great Britain in 1707
- Great Britain united with Ireland in 1801, separated from Ireland in 1922, then reincorporated 6 Irish counties in 1927
- is located on the 9th largest island of the world and the largest island of Europe
- was an agricultural society during the seventeenth century
- formed a stable government with a two-party system consisting of Conservatives and Liberals
    - Benjamin Disraeli lead the Conservatives during 1868 and the 1870's
        - Conservatives committed to laissez-faire economics (free trade with limited government interference) in the late 1800's
    - Disraeli's rival, Gladstone, led the Liberals
- the conservative view that social welfare was the responsibility of the privileged inspired passage of much humanitarian legislation, in which English conservatives usually led the way
- by the late 1800s, great conservative statesmen, notably Benjamin Disraeli, exemplified the conservative tendency to resort to moderate reform in order to preserve the foundations of the established order
- was a leader in the Industrial Revolution
    - socioeconomic benefits from emerging technologies benefited the growth and spread of the British empire
- through colonization, grew into the largest world empire, holding sway over 458 million people by 1922
- was the foremost global power for more than a century

- maintained relative stability during the French and other European revolutions, due to progressive, democratic changes in government
- fended off a proposed invasion by Napoleon when Lord Nelson defeated Napoleon at sea
  - a sense of British nationalism grew as a result of this threat
- lost hundreds of thousands of soldiers fighting for the Allied cause during World War I
- led by Winston Churchill, fought again on the Allied side during World War II
- saw many of its cities heavily damaged due to German air raids or the Luftwaffe "blitz," but eventually won the air war through the use of faster, more advanced aircraft
- shared in the World War II victory, as the Allied powers defeated the Axis powers
- experienced rapid decolonization and technological advancement after World War II
- was the first nation to suffer the difficulties associated with postindustrial development
  - Conservatives wanted to preserve private industry and advocated protective tariffs against foreign competition

France:
- one of the largest countries in Europe
- named after the Franks
- lies geographically in the shape of a hexagon
- became a more centralized state during the reign of Louis XIII (1610-1643)
- endured wars between the Catholics and Protestants (Huguenots) until the 18th century
- a major world power for more than 500 years
- experienced the impact of the Industrial Revolution, along with other European states
- colonized great parts of North America and Southeast Asia; during the 19th and early 20th centuries
- second only to Britain in size and reach of colonial empire
- was ruled by the House of Bourbon until the beheading of Louis XVI in 1793

- birthplace of the "Age of Enlightenment," a cultural movement of 18th century European and U.S. intellectuals, whose purposes included:
    - reformation of society
    - the advancement of knowledge and intellectual interchange
    - opposition to superstition, intolerance, and abuses by church and state
- Enlightenment philosophy, in which reason is advocated as the primary source for legitimacy and authority, undermined the power of and support for the monarchy, paving the way for the French Revolution
- French monarchs did not become "Enlightened Despots" (e.g. they did not embrace Enlightenment's emphasis on rationality, religious toleration, freedom of speech and the press, and the right to hold private property)
- experienced radical social and political upheaval that had a major throughout the rest of Europe with the French Revolution of 1789-1799
    - the absolute monarch that had ruled for centuries collapsed within three years
    - feudal, aristocratic and religious privileges evaporated
    - old ideas about tradition, hierarchy, monarchy, aristocracy, and religious authority) were abruptly overthrown by Enlightenment principles of equality, citizenship and inalienable rights
    - between 16,000 and 40,000 people were killed during the French Revolution's "Reign of Terror" (1793-1794), many of them by the guillotine
- during the late 1800's, utilized penal colonies in South America & the South Pacific for punishing hardened criminals that the system couldn't reform
    - because of its high mortality rate, critics of the French penal system called it a "bloodless guillotine"
    - the two most notorious French penal colonies were in New Caledonia and French Guiana
- suffered extreme casualties and material damage as a result of World War I
- felt the impact of World War I most heavily
- while still under reconstruction in the 1920s, endured severe inflation as well as other economic and social difficulties

- was ruled by the "Popular Front" prior to World War II, which came to power with a voter mandate to distribute wealth more fairly
- was rocked by economic and political difficulties prior to World War II
- despite protests from the left, compromised with Adolph Hitler and Benito Mussolini due to:
    - poor military status
    - psychological inability to handle the looming threat of war
- surrendered to Germany early in World War II (1940), and was ruled by a "collaborative government" during the war
- sent over a million French troops to help the Allied cause through the efforts of the "Free French" government
- lost more than 200,000 soldiers on the battlefields of World War II
- qualified as one of the victors of World War II due to cooperation with the Allied powers and opposition to the Nazis
- the puppet government set-up by the Nazi's was replaced by a democratic French government
- found its authority in French colonies challenged by anti-colonial movements following World War I and especially World War II
- France unsuccessfully fought bitter wars in Vietnam and Algeria to keep its empire intact
- by the end of the 1960s, many of France's colonies had gained independence

Germany:
- a democracy for the first 15 years following World War I
- became a republic and developed a constitution drawn up by the national assembly at Weimar
    - became known as the "Weimar Republic"
- suffered from the economic depression, which led to the rise of the right wing and ultimately, of Adolph Hitler
- enacted the Nuremberg Laws of 1935:
    - defined a Jew as any person with one Jewish grandparent
    - denied German citizenship to anyone defined as a Jew

Nations and Other Geographic Places

Ireland:
- island to the northwest of continental Europe
- dominated by British rule from 1603 on
- resistance to English dominance increased as a result of the potato famine, or Great Famine, which took place from 1845 to 1852
  - the Great Famine was a time of mass starvation, disease, and emigration
- English reforms in Ireland didn't satisfy Irish nationalists, who continued to struggle with the English until the outbreak of World War I
- nationalists demanded complete independence from Britain
- in 1921 the 26 southern counties became the Irish Free State
  - first called the Irish Free State, it later became the Republic of Ireland

Italy:

- country of people sharing the Italian peninsula, a common language, and historical background
- located in South-Central Europe
- consisted of a fragmented group of small kingdoms and principalities at first
- internal fighting and rivalries prevented progress and political cohesion
- Italian leaders began working towards unification, which was accomplished in 1861
- declared itself neutral at the beginning of World War I
- eventually joined the war on the side of Germany and Austria-Hungary
- suffered greatly as a result of World War I:
  - more than 650,000 Italian soldiers died
  - very few territorial gains
  - uncertain socio-economic conditions caused by war debt led to the rise to power of Fascism and the dictator, Benito Mussolini
- World War II participation resulted from imperial ambitions of the Fascist regime, which Italy joined as a member of the Axis powers (Germany, Italy, Japan)
- Fascist Italy:

- suppressed all opposition at home and threatened peace abroad
- served as a model for Nazi Germany
- was eventually forced into an alliance with Hitler which, in 1940, took Italy into World War II
- after the overthrow of Mussolini, Northern Italy became a puppet state of the Germans while southern Italy was ruled by factions that fought for the Allies
- post-war Italy evolved into the democratic republic it is today

Japan:
- island nation located in East Asia
- surrounded by the Pacific Ocean
- widened its military influence after World War I
- taken over politically by the Japanese military in the 1930s, which imposed a military dictatorship
- followed an expansionist policy, claiming the need for living space, resources, and new markets
- joined Germany as one of the Axis Powers in 1940
- attacked United States naval forces in Pearl Harbor on December 7, 1941, effectively bringing the United States into World War II
- surrendered to the Allied Powers after the 1945 atomic bombing Hiroshima and Nagasaki by the United States

Netherlands (Dutch):
- gained effective independence from Spain before the death of Philip II, though formal international recognition of that independence came only in 1648
- a geographically low-lying country, with about 20% of its area and 21% of its population located below sea level (its name literally means the "low country")
- leaders in European agricultural processes
  - created new farm plots called polders by diking and draining lands formerly under sea
- one of the first European countries to have an elected parliament (the Dutch Republic, which ruled from 1581-1795)
  - the United Provinces of Northern Netherlands resulted in a republic amid monarchies
  - though a republic, the Dutch government was far from being a truly popular democracy

Nations and Other Geographic Places

- one of the major seafaring and military powers of the 17th century, established colonies and trading posts all over the world
- explored and exploited colonies overseas through hard work and trading—despite its small size
- colonized Asia, Africa, and the Americas, in part due to its swift naval forces
    - monopolized trade and colonization in India, Indonesia, and the Philippines
- the first thoroughly capitalist country of the world, featuring an aristocratic merchant society that:
    - the economic pacesetters of seventeenth-century Europe
    - Amsterdam succeeded Antwerp as the major trading center of northwestern Europe
    - owned the East India Company, founded in 1602, which assembled and exploited a commercial empire
    - operated almost 3/4 of the world's fishing vessels
    - controlled a lucrative portion of the North Sea herring fisheries
- heavily involved in the slave trade during its colonial phase
- slow to industrialize, mainly due to the great complexity involved in modernizing the infrastructure, consisting largely of waterways, and its great reliance windpower
- not a puritanical people
- a world empire and center of international finance and culture from the late 1600s well into the 1700s
    - lost its preeminence to England in the late 1700s
    - collapsed by the end of the 18th century due to revolution and French invasion
- dominated by the French beginning in 1795, eventually being overrun by Napoleon for a short time
- became a monarchy in 1815, a few years after Napoleon had been forced to withdraw and upon the return of William I
- managed to remain neutral during World War I, though heavily involved
- declared itself neutral during World War II, but was overrun by the Germans in just five days
- post World War II, the Dutch economy prospered by leaving behind an era of neutrality and gaining closer ties with neighboring states
- is a democracy today

- considered a liberal country due to its drug policy, legalization of euthanasia, and 2001 recognition of same-sex marriage

Portugal:
- located in southwestern Europe
- pioneered the "Age of Discovery" in the 15th and 16th centuries
- became a global empire—a major economic, military, and political power—as a result of its expeditions and colonization
    - was never completely successful in their efforts to dominate the trade of Southeast Asia
    - was too small and lacked the money to maintain a foreign empire
- competed primarily with the Dutch and English in Southeast Asia
- significant losses to the Dutch during the 17th century brought an end to the Portuguese trade monopoly in the Indian Ocean
- saw Brazil, its most valuable colony, break free in 1822
- ruled by a monarch until a revolution in 1910, when the monarchy was deposed
- saw its power diminish until it was not a major player, or power, in World War I or World War II
    - fought with the Allies in World War I
    - was ruled by a pro-Fascist government during World War II
        - exported goods to both sides during the war
        - eventually sided with the Allies
- ruled by a democratic republic in modern times

Russia:
- located in Northern Eurasia
- largest country in the world, covering more than one eighth of the Earth's inhabited land area
- spans nine time zones and has the world's largest reserves of mineral and energy resources
- ruled by the Czars until the Russian Revolution (1917)
- endured economic disaster, which resulted partly from the inability of Czar Nicholas I (who ruled from 1825-1855) to see the weaknesses within Austrian and Prussian alliances

Nations and Other Geographic Places

- Czar Alexander II (Nicholas I's successor, who ruled from 1855-1891) was forced to realize that that Russia was no longer a great military power
    - Alexander II's advisors argued that Russia's serf-based economy could no longer compete with industrialized nations
        - serfs were peasants bound to the land and (to some extent) their owners
- Czar Nicholas II set up a legislative body known as the Duma in 1906
    - despite instituting the Duma, Nicholas II refused to relinquish autocratic control
    - the first two parliaments didn't last long, accomplished nothing, and were dissolved within a year by Nicholas II due to impasses between the Duma and the Czar's government, and lack of productivity
    - the third state Duma was more successful and actually served its full five year term
- slow to adopt the Industrial Revolution
- capitalism was rapidly developing in Russia by the time the third and fourth Dumas were convened
- Russia entered World War I (in which 3.3 million Russians were killed) in 1914
- Czar Nicholas II abdicated in 1917 as a result of the Russian Revolution, and was killed the following year
- following the Russian Revolution, Russia became the largest and leading constituent of the Soviet Union

Soviet Union
- the world's first constitutionally socialist state and a recognized superpower
- was the world's largest country
- played a decisive role in the Allied victory in World War II
- saw some of the most significant technological achievements of the 20th century, including the world's first human spaceflight
- existed from 1922 to 1991
- Vladimir Lenin was the first leader of the Soviet Union
- Joseph Stalin assumed rule after Lenin died in the 1920s, and was the was its most famous leader

- Stalin was famous for his brutality—he sent many Russians to concentration camps
- the "Great Purge" happened in the 1930s—hundreds of thousands of people were executed
- even though Germany had a peace treaty with the Soviet Union, Germany broke the treaty and invaded Russia in 1941
- German soldiers suffered from Russia's cold weather and were driven all the way back to Berlin by the time the war was over
- over 27 million Russians died in World War II
- despite the World War II losses, the Soviet Union remained a World Super Power for over four decades
- the Cold War happened from the 1950s to the 1990s—where the United States clashed with Russia over communist influence in the world and nuclear weapon pileups
- the Cold War was a non-violent war
- Mikhail Gorbachev came to power in the 1980s and brought many democratic reforms to Russia

Spain
- was the Europe's leading power throughout the 16th century and most of the 17th century
- was a leader in the Age of Discovery, where ships sailed around the world to claim lands for the Spanish Empire and the Catholic Church
- the Spanish Empire included great parts of the Americas, islands in the Asia-Pacific area, parts of Italy, cities in Northern Africa, and parts of other European Countries
- the Protestant Reformation weakened France, and lead to wars based on religious differences
- Spain went into a decline in the late 1700s when it surrendered a number of small territories to France, however, it maintained its vast overseas empire until the early 1800s
- in the late 1930s there was the Spanish Civil War, which caused 500,000 deaths and lead to 500,000 Spanish citizens leaving the country
- declared itself neutral at the beginning of World War I and remained so throughout the whole war, although sympathetic to the Axis powers

- after World War II, Spain was politically and economically isolated, and was kept out of the United Nations

United States:
- was deeply influenced by the Age of Enlightenment and Industrial Revolution
- originally favored isolationism and tried to stay neutral during World War I
- dramatically expanded its government in response to World War I
- played a vital role in the conclusion of that war
- colonized the Philippines and Hawaii
- entered World War II after the Japanese attack on Pearl Harbor on December 7, 1941
- fought with the Allied Forces during World War II
- helped end the war by dropping two atomic bombs on Japan
- followed World War II with the Cold War against Russia

Battles and Wars

American Revolution (1775-1783):
- war for independence from England fought by the 13 colonies of the United States

Battle of Trafalgar (1805):
- naval engagement fought by the British against the combined fleets of the French and the Spanish
- decisively won by the English, and served to establish their naval supremacy in years to come

Crimean War (1853-1856):
- originated over what became known as the Eastern Question:
  - "Who would benefit most from the disintegration of the Ottoman Empire?"
- Russia desired to expand its territory at the expense of the Ottoman Empire
- France and England feared an upset in the delicate balance of power together with a scramble for pieces of the Ottoman Empire
- While the Ottoman Empire rapidly declined in the 19th century (starting in the 1820s):
  - France and England worked to keep it alive
    - they wanted to preserve commercial opportunities and naval bases in the eastern Mediterranean

Franco-Vietnamese War, or First Indochina War (1946-1954):
- an uprising by the Vietnamese against French authority after World War II
- reached a turning point after the fierce battle and French defeat at Dien Bien Phu
  - the French wanted the war to end
  - the battle led to the Geneva Conference and Geneva Accords of 1954 and a realignment of world politics
  - Vietnam was organized into the North and South by the Geneva Conference

French Revolution (1789-1799:
- resulted in the spread of liberalism and the revolution principles of liberty, equality, and fraternity throughou as French armies destabilized foreign monarchies and s governments

Korean War (1950-1953):
- began on June 25, 1950 when Soviet-armed North Korean troops:
    - crossed the 38th parallel
    - invade the Republic of Korea
- first major military conflict of the Cold War
- first in a string of small but bloody battles around the world fought to contain Communism

Napoleonic Wars (1803-1815):
- a series of wars declared against Napoleon's French empire by opposing coalitions
- aroused a spirit of nationalism throughout Europe as the French made themselves hated oppressors
- ultimately resulted in complete military defeat for Napoleon

Peninsular War (1808-1814):
- the Spanish people successfully resisted Napoleonic conquest
- bands of Spanish guerrillas took control of large areas of the countryside, attacking French troops, supply lines and couriers
- the revolt spread throughout the country
- resulted in the ouster of the French from Spain in 1814

Russian Revolution of 1905:
- began in St. Petersburg
- troops fired on a defenseless crowd of workers who, led by a priest, were marching to the Winter Palace to petition Czar Nicholas II

Russian Revolution of 1917:
- a backlash against centuries of:
    - autocratic and repressive czarist rule
    - severe economic and social conditions for the general populace
- fomented by various 19th and 20th century movements to overthrow the government staged by students, peasants, or nobles
- came to a head with a mounting wave of food and wave strikes in Petrograd in 1917
    - February 23 demonstrations involved 90,000 people
    - the principle slogan was the demand for bread
    - despite numerous encounters with police, the workers continued to occupy the streets and refused to disperse
- after achieving success in Petrograd, quickly spread in the same manner throughout the country
- resulted in the creation of two parallel systems of government
    - Soviets functioned side by side with authorities who communicated with the Provisional Government

Seven Years' War (1756-1763):
- often seen as a continuation of the War of Austrian Succession
- indicative of the weaknesses of the Hapsburg dynastic empire.
- marked by Britain's control over India and the end of France's "Old Empire"
- complex in its origin and involved two main distinct conflicts
    - the colonial rivalry between France and England
    - the struggle for supremacy in Germany between the house of Austria and the rising kingdom of Prussia

Battles and Wars

Spanish-American War (1898):
- fought between Spain and the United States over continued U.S. intervention in the Cuban War of Independence
- angered over reports of Spanish atrocities in Cuba, Americans closely watched the Cuban uprisings against the Spanish for decades
- the mysterious 1898 sinking of the battleship *Maine* at Havana Harbor triggered the war

Thirty Years War (1618-1648):
- triggered by disagreement about the meaning of The Peace of Augsburg
- began with the rebellion of Bohemian Protestant nobles (which were under Hapsburg domination) against King Ferdinand I (a Catholic)
- fought primarily over Catholic and Protestant religious differences
    - also important in determining the political future of the Hapsburg line
- fought mostly in Germany
- ended as a political struggle to reduce the power of the Hapsburgs in favor of France and Sweden

World War I (1914-1918):
- initially triggered in 1914 when Hapsburg archduke Francis Ferdinand, heir to the throne of Austria-Hungary, was assassinated in the streets of Sarajevo
    - Ferdinand was assassinated by a Serbian nationalist
    - Bosnia had long been coveted by the Serbs
    - the Austria-Hungary government issued a severe ultimatum in response to the assassination
    - the Serbian government refused to accept the ultimatum entirely
    - as a result, Austria declared war on Serbia on July 28
- was really caused by:
    - the military alliance of two powerful countries (Italy and Germany) which altered the delicate balance of power in Europe

- o the rise of nationalism in European countries
  - German nationalism fostered Nazism
  - Italian nationalism led to Fascism
  - the Serbs wanted to stamp out Bosnian nationalism, which they viewed as responsible for the assassination
  - Russia entered the war as a supporter of Serbian nationalism
- was entered by the United States in 1917 due to:
  - o Germany's resumption of U-Boat submarine warfare by attacking merchant convoys and ships (primary reason)
  - o fear for national security if Germany won the war (secondary reason)
  - o profits to be made (secondary reason)
- strongly influenced demographic trends
- claimed the lives of more than 9 million soldiers
- caused even more significant deaths through malnutrition and war-related disease (as many as 36 million people)
- the population also suffered from birth deficits as a result of economic dislocation
- destroyed an entire generation of young men, potential leaders in industry and politics, in Britain and France
- marked the first use of trench warfare as a central feature of military conflict
  - o invention of rapid-firing small arms and artillery made the infantry charges of earlier wars virtually impossible
  - o as the war became immobile, armies dug thousands of miles of opposing trenches fronted by barbed wire
- resulted in a major influx of women into the workforce in France, England, and the U.S.
  - o women performed jobs that only men had performed before
  - o in Britain alone, almost 1.5 million women were hired for war-time jobs
  - o after the war women were expected to quit their jobs and make way for the men returning home
    - governments moved quickly to remove women from the workforce by lowering salaries and reducing or eliminating benefits

World War II (1939-1945):
- was the second global conflict
- resulted from the rise of totalitarian, militaristic regimes in Germany, Italy, and Japan
    - which rose out of the economic crisis of Great Depression and conditions created by the peace settlements of World War I, which imposed crushing financial burdens on the losing countries
- began on September 1, 1939, when Germany, without a declaration of war, invaded Poland
- escalated on September 3, 1939, which Britain and France declared war on Germany
    - all the Commonwealth of Nations, except Ireland, rapidly followed suit.
- Germany quickly conquered Poland
    - The German blitzkrieg, or lightning war, with its use of new techniques of mechanized and air warfare, crushed the Polish defenses
    - Germany's conquest was almost complete when Soviet forces entered Poland
- Hitler and Stalin signed the Russo-German pact in 1939
    - this pact disillusioned Communists around the world
    - permanently derailed the Communist movement, which was already reeling
    - led many intellectuals to look for another place on the political spectrum—besides communism
- The United States was determined to maintain neutrality
    - was drawn closer and closer to war by the force of events
    - voted to aid Britain in 1941 to save them from collapse
    - entered the war officially after December 7, 1941, after Japan attacked Pearl Harbor
        - The U.S. had gained Hawaiian rights in 1887, when the Hawaiian monarchy permitted a coaling and repair station
        - After the U.S. annexed Hawaii in 1898, Pearl Harbor became a naval base
- By 1941, the Axis Powers controlled almost all of Europe, and busily:

- exploited the economic and human resources of the conquered lands
- persecuted Jews in the occupied lands, sending millions to their deaths in concentration camps
  - Nazi resistance movements still existed in most countries
- The Japanese:
  - followed their attack on Pearl Harbor with lightning assaults across the Pacific, capturing:
    - Hong Kong from the British
    - the Philippines from the United States
    - many other islands
- The United States:
  - punished Japan with many bombing raids, which took a heavy toll
  - urged the Japanese to surrender
  - utilized the atomic bomb (under the leadership of President Harry Truman) when the Japanese refused to surrender
    - President Truman wanted to save Allied lives by ending the war as soon as possible
    - the bombs were dropped on Hiroshima and Nagasaki in early August, 1945, killing tens of thousands of people
    - the Japanese surrendered on August 14, ending World War II

Eras and Movements

Age of Enlightenment (circa 1650—1700 thru circa 1789—1815):
- an intellectual movement
- greatest development occurred during the 18th century
- started between 1650 and 1700 A.D., ended between 1789 and 1815 (there is little consensus among historians about the exact dates)
- developed simultaneously in many European countries and spread across much of the western world
- a time of reason, natural law, and progress
- heavily questioned the political and social norms of the day
- led people to seek self-governance with an emphasis on liberty and individual rights
- triggered government reforms designed to stamp out unequal treatment before the law and preserve rights and property
- fostered the beliefs that:
    - human reason could remedy problems of the past and create a Utopian government
    - humans could correct the errors of their ways if the errors were pointed out to them
- changed how people thought about enjoying their lives
    - began focusing on how to enjoy their time on earth instead of suffering now in order to enjoy the afterlife
- influenced monarchs who were enlightened and absolutist to declare themselves servants of the state or people, instead of proclaiming the divine right to rule
- greatly influenced the Constitution of the United States, which embodies the ideals of the Enlightenment
- became known as the "The Age of Reason" in its later stages
- lost momentum in Europe when the continent became preoccupied with the French Revolution
- came under increasing attack for being too rational simple

The Great Fear (July 20-August 5, 1789 in France):

- a revolt in the French countryside at the start of the French Revolution, triggered by rumors that armed men (brigands) were coming to take their food
- brigands were aristocratic hirelings who destroyed ripe crops and forced the National Assembly to preserve the status quo

The October Days (1789, French Revolution):
- drought crippled the operation of the watermills for grinding flour from the wheat
- Parisians lined up for bread and remained suspicious of the royal troops stationed near the city

Reign of Terror (1793-1794, French Revolution):
- occurred just four years after the French Revolution started
- marked by an acceleration of arrests and the execution of more than 40,000 victims
- led by Robespierre and his Committee of Public Safety
- the inhumanity of the "Reign of Terror" prompted one historian to describe it as "a political philosophy written in blood"

The Scientific Revolution:
- occurred in the 16th and 17th centuries
- brought many advances in astronomy and physics
- featured huge contributions to astronomy and physics by Copernicus, Galileo, and Newton
  - many of their discoveries, which formed the foundations of modern science, contradicted leading scientific "facts" of the time

Thermidorean Reaction (1794, French Revolution):
- was a revolt against the excesses of the Reign of Terror during the French Revolution
- was triggered by a vote of the National Convention to execute Maximilien Robespierre and other leaders of the French Revolution
- The leaders of the Thermidorean Reaction, or the move toward moderation, dismantled the machinery of the Terror
- many were former Jacobins, and they disbanded the Revolutionary Tribunal, recalled the deputies on mission, and

deprived the Committees of Public Safety and General Security of their independent authority
- took the first step toward restoring Catholicism by permitting priests to celebrate mass
    - were able to practice under state supervision and without state financial support
- the press and the theatre had recovered their freedom, and pleasure seekers again flocked to Paris, now liberated from the somber Republic of Virtue
- concluded with the passage of the constitution of 1795, which was the last major act of the Convention
- supporters wanted both to retain the republic and assure the dominance of the propertied classes
- the new constitution denied the right to vote to the poorest quarter of the nation

Political Alliances, Documents, and Treaties
In Chronological Order

Hanseatic League (13th to 17th centuries):
- alliance of German cities and their merchant guilds that dominated trade along the coast of Northern Europe.
- founded in the 13th century
- grew to include more than 80 cities by 1500 A.D. (including the leading cities of Sweden, Norway, and Denmark)

Peace of Augsburg (1555):
- treaty intended to end the religious struggle between German Catholics and Protestants
- permanently divided Germany into Lutheran and Catholic faiths
- enacted in 1555 A.D.
- recognized Lutherans and Catholics, but excluded all other religions
- did not bring complete religious peace to Germany because it failed to recognize Calvinism

Protestant Union (1608):
- alliance of German Protestant leaders of cities and states
- formed by Calvinist princes who sponsored active missions in both Lutheran and Catholic regions
- founded for the avowed purpose of defending the lands, person, and rights of each individual member

Catholic League (1609):
- formed in response to the Calvinists' sponsorship of missions by the Catholic German states
- initiated by Duke Maximilian in 1608 when he started negotiations with the spiritual electors and the Catholic states of the empire
- created with a view to the formation of a union of the Catholic states

Political Alliances, Documents, and Treaties

- formed to oppose the Protestant Union (which had organized in 1608)

English Navigation Acts (started in 1651):
- a series of laws that restricted the use of foreign shipping for trade between England and its colonies
- designed to force colonial development into lines favorable to England and stop direct colonial trade with the Netherlands, France and other European countries
- were based on a mercantilist economic theory in Britain
- limited American trade by requiring the colonies to move their goods in British ships and to send certain goods directly to Britain
- were revoked once Britain switched to a policy of free trade

Treaty of Utrecht (1713):
- ended the War of Spanish Succession, which had started in 1702
  - fought on land and at sea
  - battles took place in Spain, Italy, Holland, Germany, Belgium, and France
  - put an end to the ambitious plans of Louis XIV
- restored the international balance of power
- strategic concerns came into play as imperial powers sought to protect trade routes
- made England the supreme naval power of the world
- resulted in land gains for the Austrians, the Dutch, and the English
- resulted in land losses for the French
- the Spanish King Phillip V got to keep his colonies
- England gained the very profitable right to transport slaves into Spanish America

Declaration of Independence (1776):
- created by the Americans
- adopted by representatives of the 13 North American colonies
- signed when the 13 colonies separated from Great Britain
- embodied the Enlightenment by listing the pursuit of happiness as a fundamental human right

Edict of Toleration (1787):
- the Edict of Toleration restored the civil rights of French Protestants, which annoyed the clergy

Estates-General of 1789:
- summoned by Louis XVI:
- consisted of peers and deputies from towns and provinces across France
- was intended to give the people a voice in French government
- had not convened since 1614
- failed when the people realized that the real focus was on raising taxes rather than representation
- was convened too late to stop the French revolution
- Louis XVI was beheaded three years later

Tennis Court Oath (1789):
- a pivotal event during the first days of the French Revolution
- deputies from the third estate (commoners & peasants) met on a tennis court in Versailles and swore never to disband until France had a constitution
- Louis XVI replied by commanding each estate to resume its separate deliberations
- the third estate and some deputies disobeyed at first
- Louis XVI gave in to the reformers when he saw that he couldn't trust his royal troops
- Louis XVI replaced the estates with a National Assembly, which included everybody and a constitution
- the destruction of the Bastille signified the fall of the Old Regime

Declaration of the Rights of Man (1789):
- was a fundamental document of the French Revolution
- was a charter of basic liberties inspired by the American Declaration of Independence
- the document promised liberty, property, security and resistance to oppression
- Freedom from arbitrary arrest as well as freedom of speech and the press were also promised
- said all citizens had the right to be free according to law
- mirrored the economic and political attitudes of the middle class

- said each citizen could be involved in the government through their own means or via representation
- was attractive to many aristocrats because it insisted on the sanctity of property, even though it said that social distinctions be only used for usefulness

Civil Constitution of the Clergy (June 1790):
- French Revolution document that redrew the ecclesiastical map of France
- reduced the number of bishoprics by more than a third
- made the remaining dioceses correspond to new civil administrative units
- a new bishop was required to take an oath of loyalty to the state
- the Civil Constitution stipulated that he might not apply to the pope for confirmation, though he might write to him as the visible head of the Universal Church
- these provisions stripped the pope of effective authority of French clergy and ran counter to the tradition of the Roman church as an ecclesiastical monarchy
- was the first great blunder of the Revolution
- when the National Assembly required that every member of the French clergy take a special oath supporting the Civil Constitution, only a few bishops and fewer than half of all priests complied
- the National Assembly voted to confiscate the land owned by the Catholic Church and sell it at public auction
- many who had supported previous reforms introduced by the assembly could not accept this reform of the Church and turned against the Revolution.

French Constitution of 1791:
- created two classes of citizens, active and passive
- limited the right of voting to those citizens who annually paid in taxes an amount equal to at least 3 days' wages for unskilled labor in their locality
- the passive citizens numbered a third of the male population and enjoyed full protection of the law, but were not able to vote
- active citizens voted for electors who were required to be men of substantial wealth and who ultimately elected the deputies
- it was still assumed that property determined political wisdom

Congress of Vienna (1815):
- resulted in the creation of the kingdom of Netherlands
- combined two states with different languages, religions, customs and traditions (Belgium and Holland)
- was intended to block further French expansion after the defeat of Napoleon

Durham Report (1839):
- Britain's solution to pacify the North American provinces
- drafted by Lord Durham
- proposed a union of the British and French portions of Canada
- would have granted full responsible government to the united colony

Balfour Declaration (1917):
- created a Jewish homeland in Palestine
- was the first step towards the creation of the modern state of Israel
- began with a letter from the British Foreign Secretary, Arthur Balfour, and eventually became part of a treaty

Paris Peace Conference (1919):
- convened on January 18, 1919
- dominated by discussions about land transfers and war reparations
- comprised a meeting of the Allied victors following the end of World War I to set peace terms for the defeated Central Powers
- was ineffective at establishing peace because:
  - Germans felt they had no say in any aspect of proposed treaties
  - Russia (under Bolshevik power) was not invited to the tables of the conference
- resulted, after six months of negotiations, in the Treaty of Versailles

Political Alliances, Documents, and Treaties

Treaty of Versailles (1919):
- officially ended World War I
- created two new countries out of what used to be the Austro-Hungarian Empire
    - Czechoslovakia
    - Hungary
- formed other countries due to land lost by Russia
    - Poland
    - Lithuania
    - Latvia
    - Estonia
    - Finland
- included a "War Guilt" clause which required war reparations from Germany, Austria, Hungary, Bulgaria, and Turkey
- Germany was seen to be the chief aggressor in the war
    - Germany's debt to the world was deemed to include not only money, but intellectual property, coal, and steel
    - it was the German reparations that would eventually disturb the peace and economy of the world, again
    - German nationals were humiliated and enraged over the suffering and shame imposed by the Treaty of Versailles
    - the foundation of Hitler's rise to power was laid by the treatment Germany received from the Allied Powers after the war, and in the German desire for revenge
    - terms of the Treaty of Versailles were punitive, including punishments that were both material and symbolic in nature
    - Hitler's rise to power was based on his ability to reconstruct the German identity through a sense of nationalistic pride.

League of Nations (1919):
- an international organization designed to serve as a permanent consultation system
- initially composed of the victors and a few neutrals
- brainchild of U. S. President Woodrow Wilson
- adopted, after much persuasion, at the Paris Peace Conference

Dawes Plan (1924):
- resulted after World War I, when an economic depression struck all of Europe

- - - Germany pleaded for a moratorium or delay on reparations payments
    - France would not agree
    - Germany eventually had to default on its payments
  - reduced the yearly payments Germany owed
  - granted Germany a loan on war reparation payments

Allied Powers of World War II (1939-1945):
- countries that opposed the Axis powers during the Second World War
- at the start of the war (1939), the anti-German coalition consisted of France, Poland and the United Kingdom
- they were soon joined by the British dominions of Australia, Canada, New Zealand, and South Africa
- later Allies included the United States of America, Soviet Union, China, Belgium, Brazil, Czechoslovakia, Ethiopia, Greece, India, the Netherlands, and Norway
- were led by Winston Churchill (Great Britain), Joseph Stalin (Soviet Union), and Franklin Roosevelt (United States)
  - these powers and their leaders became known as the "Big Three"
  - they met throughout the war to plan strategy and discuss postwar policy
  - cooperation between the "Big Three" ended after World War II when the "Cold War" between the western democracies and Soviet Union began
  - met in Yalta (southern Russia) in 1948
    - agreed that eastern European governments were to be freely elected (but pro-Russian)
- began with the Triple Entente, an alliance of increasingly armed nations that had formed by the beginning of the 20th century
  - included France, Britain, and Russia
  - was politically opposed by the Triple Entente (Germany, Austria-Hungary, and Italy)
- Russia, England and France:
  - had only recently come together as close allies
  - each had many sources of conflict with its allies
  - shared no common language and held no mutual cooperation

Political Alliances, Documents, and Treaties

Axis Powers of World War II (1939-1945):

- the alignment of nations that fought in the Second World War against the Allied forces
- was first known as the Triple Alliance, a group of increasingly armed nations that had formed by the beginning of the 20th century
    - included Germany, Austria-Hungary, and Italy
    - was politically opposed by the Triple Entente (France, Britain, and Russia)
- Germany signed treaties with Italy and Japan in 1936
- the Axis Pact, which included Germany, Italy, and Japan, was signed in 1940
- at one point the Soviet Union was part of the alliance
- at their zenith during World War II, the Axis powers presided over empires that occupied large parts of the world
- the war ended in 1945 with the defeat of the Axis powers and the dissolution of the alliance
- like the Allies, membership of the Axis was fluid, with nations entering and leaving over the course of the war

Marshall Plan (1947):
- developed when U.S. Secretary of State George C. Marshall urged that European countries decide on their economic needs so that material and financial aid from the United States could be integrated on a broad scale
- was administered by the Economic Cooperation Administration (ECA), which was established in April of 1948 by President Truman

Truman Doctrine (1947):
- American policy of providing economic and military aid to Greece and Turkey because they were threatened by communism.
- resulted when Greece was threatened with a communist revolution in and the Soviet Union began making demands on Turkey
- an aggressive foreign policy aimed at curbing the spread of Communism

North Atlantic Treaty Organization, NATO (1949):
- established to defend Western Europe against Stalinist Russia
- formed by the western allies
- one of the major Western countermeasures in the cold war against the threat of aggression by the Soviet Union
- aimed at safeguarding the freedom of the Atlantic community
- provided for collective self-defense
- considered an armed attack on any member an attack against all

Warsaw Pact (began in 1955):
- a mutual defense treaty between eight communist states of Eastern Europe in existence during the Cold War
- enforced Soviet policy within her East European satellites

Political and Cultural Forces

Bolsheviks:
- Russian political party that returned from exile and formed in 1903
- came to power with the Russian Revolution of 1917
- demanded that Russia participate in general peace negotiations
- were dominated by Vladimir Lenin, who quickly converted the party to his course
- under the leadership of Lenin, began to press for:
    - assumption of full power by the Soviets
    - immediate termination of the war
    - seizure of land by the peasants
    - control of the workers through industrial production

Divine Right monarchies (17th-18th centuries):
- dated back to when several monarchs in Europe (particularly England and France) increased the power of their central governments
    - each leader came to power based on powers obtained through God
    - the monarchies were "Absolute"
    - +*monarchs claimed that they ruled by divine right and answered to no one except God
- was seen as a logica extension of the Gallicanism of Louis XIV
    - Gallicanism favored a restraint of the pope's authority in the Church to that of the bishops and the temporal ruler
    - Louis XIV believed himself to be a representative of God on earth
- chief opposition consisted of feudal nobles
- early anti-monarchist publications in England were published in the mid to late sixteenth century after Mary I succeeded her brother, Edward VI

French Middle Class:
- the urban workers and the bourgeouisie of the French Revolution
- the other members of the third estate besides the peasants

- became increasingly frustrated and alienated at the decreasing wages and their growing economic disadvantage
- wealthier, better-educated, and more articulate than the peasants and wage earners
- took the lead in formulating the grievances of the entire third estate
- found it appalling to be snubbed by the nobility and treated as second-class citizens of the monarchy, in addition to being denied posts of power in the government, church, and army

French Union (1946-1958):
- a political party created to replace the colonial system
- established by the French Constitution in 1946
- included France and her former colonies

Girondins:
- the majority party during the French Revolution
    - capable politicians of the left who captured the votes of the Plain
    - a loose grouping of Jacobins
- called Girondins because many of them came from Bordeaux, in the department of Gironde
- driven to enact different pieces of drastic legislation, most notably the Civil Constitution of the Clergy, which weakened their own position
- held together by their patriotic alarm over France's situation at home and abroad
- failed to develop an effective party organization
- were opposed by the Jacobins, the radical minority
- favored a large measure of federalism in the government
    - at that time, federalism meant decentralization and a national government limited by many checks and balances
- led by their chief spokesman, Jacques Brissot
    - an ambitious lawyer, journalist, and champion of reform causes, including the emancipation of slaves
- united with another faction, the Mountains, to declare France a republic on September 21, 1792
- came mainly from middle class professions, and, like the Mountains, were steeped in the ideas of the philosophes

Political and Cultural Forces

House of Bourbon (16th-18th centuries):
- line of kings who ruled France from the 16th to the 18th century
- overthrown in the French Revolution with the execution of Louis XVI
- later attempts at reinstatement were not permanent

Jacobins:
- radical minority party during the French Revolution
- wanted to abolish the monarchy and set up a republic based on universal suffrage (right to vote)
- led by Jean Paul Marat, an embittered Swiss physician turned journalist, who continually excited the people of Paris
  - Marat was later murdered in his bathtub by a Girondin sympathizer, Charlotte Corday

Mountains:
- a faction with ties to the Jacobins
- united with the Girondins to declare France a republic on September 21, 1792
- were named because they sat high up in the meeting hall
- came mainly from middle class professions, and, like the Girondins, were steeped in the ideas of the philosophes

Old Hapsburg Empire:
- one of the most important royal houses of Europe (House of Hapsburg)
- origin of all the formally elected Holy Roman Emperors between 1438 and 1740, plus rulers of Austria, Spain, and several other countries
- was complete broken up by the end of World War I
  - Charles I came to the throne in 1916
  - his attempts at peace negotiations were unsuccessful
  - the empire was dismembered during his rule

Old Regime (15th-18th centuries):
- term used to describe the institutions prevailing in Europe, especially France, before 1789
  - Louis XV refused to take decisive steps to remedy the abuses associated with the Old Regime

- - commoners in France under Louis XV struggled to overcome social barriers in its rigid colonial system
- was supported by three estates:
  - First estate: the clergy
    - occupied a position of conspicuous importance in France
    - though only .5% of the population, controlled 15% of the land
    - performed public functions such as keeping vital statistics (births and deaths), giving relief to the poor, and overseeing public education
  - Second estate: the nobility
  - Third estate: commoners or peasants
    - included over 97% of the French population

Philosophes (1740-1793):
- a French word
- referred to the intellectuals of the Enlightenment—the critics, publicists, economists, and political scientists, who:
  - focused their work on the Encyclopédie, which when completed, it contained twenty-two volumes of text and eleven of art
  - viewed the minds of the young as "blank slates", and sought to find the best way to fill them
    - this theory is known as Tabula Rasa, and is a key belief of empiricism
  - accepted the "Newtonian world-machine" view of the universe (also known as Deism), which teaches that:
    - God set the universe in motion and then let it continue on its own
    - God acts as an absentee landlord
    - God does not intervene in human affairs
    - miracles don't occur
    - the world operates by natural and self-sustaining laws
    - the Bible is a historical document but not divinely inspired
  - found part of their motivation in the writings of French philosopher René Descartes

Political and Cultural Forces

Physiocrats (second half of 18th century):
- school of 18th century French thinkers who evolved the first complete system of economics
- believed in the rule of nature
- regarded agriculture rather than trade as the key to national wealth
- proposed that a nation's wealth should be measured in agricultural production rather than gold
- opposed mercantilism
- held that economic growth required free markets

Sans-culottes:
- the bulk of the common people during the French Revolution
- a group of men and women united by the common fear that they would starve because they couldn't buy bread
- the name means "those without knee breeches"
- were once divided groups, but united due to common economic concerns

Tories (18th-19th centuries):
- British political party that was most powerful in the 18th and 19th centuries
- began in 1678 with a group which opposed the Exclusion Bill and sought to exclude James, Duke of York, from ascending to the throne of England because he was Catholic
- focused on upholding the traditional political structure and the established church

Tudor Dynasty (1485-1603):
- also known as the House of Tudor
- ruled England and its realms from 1485 through 1603
- was succeeded by the House of Stuart in 1603, when Elizabeth I died without providing an heir

Whigs (18th-19th centuries):
- British political party
- focused on limiting royal authority and increase parliamentary power

Political, Philosophical, and Scientific Ideas

Anti-Semitism:
- was fanned by the migration of the poorer Jews from regions of eastern Europe
- was common in Austria
- developed partly out of religious prejudice and partly out of distaste for liberal politics preferred by the Jewish middle-class

Anarchy:
- opposition to any form of government
- belief that no government is just
- no government at all seen as the ideal situation

Autocracy:
- form of government which resides in the absolute, unlimited power of a single individual
- established in Russia when the nation was illiterate, uneducated, and attempting to ward off foreign attacks from all sides
- seen as a God-given right by Alexander III, Tsar of Russia

Collectivization:
- was a policy enacted by Joseph Stalin
- forced peasants and farmers to surrender their land and livestock and join collective farms administered by the communist government
- was an economic disaster in both the short and long-term
- resulted in the starvation of an estimated 10 million people starved to death, as collectives:
    o were poorly managed and listlessly farmed
    o became the Achilles heel of the Soviet Union until its disintegration in 1991

Political, Philosophical, and Scientific Ideas

Colonialism:
- movement in the late 1800 and 1930 by which Western nations acquired 84% of the world's land
  - resulted in European states amassing vast political empires, mainly in Africa but also in Asia
  - Britain dominated India after 1815
    - India became the symbol of empire when Disraeli had Queen Victoria proclaimed empress of India
  - France acquired a colonial empire in North Africa and Indochina in the 1800's
    - French Indochina, the richest and most prestigious of France's possessions, included Laos, Cambodia, and three Vietnamese colonies (Annam, Tonkin, and Cochin China)
- powered by economic, political, and psychological motives
  - competition for trade
  - protection of trade routes
  - superior military force
  - European power politics
  - a belief in European superiority
- bitterly criticized by some Europeans as a betrayal of the Western ideals of freedom and equality

Conservatism:
- emerged in the 19th century
- a reaction to the political and social changes resulting from the French and Industrial Revolutions
- promoted the:
  - preserving of the power of kings and aristocrats
  - maintaining landholder influence against the rising industrial bourgeoisie
  - limiting suffrage
  - continuing ties between church and state
- originated with Edmund Burke's famous 1790 book *Reflections on the Revolution in France*, which promoted the ideas that society is:
  - a contract, nothing more than a partnership agreement between a government and its citizens
  - by nature a temporary arrangement which can be dissolved

Deduction (Deductive Reasoning):
- process of using a general truth to produce a specific conclusion
  - medieval mode of reasoning
  - develops from the general expectation to the particular example as proof
- sometimes contrasted with inductive reasoning

Despotism:
- form of government featuring a single, absolute ruler
- proposed by advocates of enlightened despotism as a shortcut to utopia, where tyrants could become benevolent reformers
- now holds a negative context

Existentialism:
- major philosophical movement that centered on the individual and his relationship to the universe or to God
- resulted from the traumas of war and the subsequent questioning of conventional religions
- made popular by the philosopher Jean-Paul Sartre (Kierkegaard is considered the founder of modern existentialism)

Imperialism (late 19th century):
- when Western powers acquired both formal and informal empires, exercising control over areas that were technically independent
- closely tied to nationalism
- intense competition among the nations of Europe created a demand to acquire foreign colonies that provided coaling stations and sea ports for their navies
- colonies produced valuable raw materials such as tin, rubber and oil not available in Western countries control of these raw materials offered an economic motivation to promote imperialism

Political, Philosophical, and Scientific Ideas

Induction (Inductive Reasoning):
- scientific reasoning that develops from a particular observed phenomenon which may be parlayed into a general conclusion
- forms a general theory or idea about how things work based on an observed result
- is the opposite of deduction or deductive reasoning
- introduced by Francis Bacon

Isolationism:
- national policy of isolation from the affairs of other nations by declining to enter into alliances, foreign economic commitments, foreign trade, etc.
- devoting the entire efforts of one's country to its own advancement
- seeking to remain at peace by avoiding foreign entanglements and responsibilities
- acted out by the United States when it attempted to remain involved in world politics without a real commitment
- allowed the U. S. to continue the belief that they were practicing legalism and not in any danger of attack

Laissez Faire:
- means "Live and let live"
- the liberal doctrine of a free economy in France
  - free economy activists in the United States today are often associated with the Libertarian political party

Liberalism:
- assumes that people, having a rational intellect, will recognize problems and solve them
- has a characteristic belief in human goodness and rationality
- was the political leaning of most middle class men during the mid-1800s
- promoted the concepts of:
  - protection of civil liberties
  - freedom of assembly
  - freedom of speech and press
  - equality under the law
  - freedom from arbitrary arrest

- - limiting the right to vote & hold office to those who owned property
- discouraged:
  - universal suffrage
  - equal political rights
  - sharing power with the lower classes

Mercantilism:
- economic system utilized by many major trading nations in Europe up to the 18th century
- emphasized exporting as much as possible and importing as little as possible
- aimed to collect as much gold as possible and increase national wealth through regulation of all commercial interests
- later replaced by laissez-faire (free market) economics
- successfully promoted by the Frenchman Jean-Baptiste Colbert

National Patriotism:
- the expression of nationalistic pride in one's own country and culture
- rose to popularity around the time when Spain, France, and England became world powers
- typically develops out of a need for a sense of unity with others in one's homeland

Nationalism:
- the most successful political force of the 19th century
- emerged from two main sources:
  - the Romantic exaltation of "feeling" and "identity"
  - the Liberal requirement that a legitimate state be based on a "people" rather than a dynasty, God, or imperial domination
- heavily influenced both the German and Italian states after 1815
  - divided nations (Germany, Italy, and Hungary) wanted their own nation states with centralized governments

Political, Philosophical, and Scientific Ideas

Nazism:
- political ideology of Adoph Hitler and Nazi Germany
- abolished all labor unions in 1933
- abolished employer's associations in 1934
- replaced labor unions and employer's associations with a "Labor Front" that include all wage earners, salaried persons, professionals, and employers
- forbade strikes and lockouts
- promised jobs to workers as long as they accepted the system
- implemented racism as part of state policy
- boycotted the businesses and professions of the Jews
- outlawed Jews from holding public office, flying the national flag, writing, publishing, exhibiting paintings, giving concerts, working as a professional, or working in hospitals, banks, or schools

New Imperialism:
- the late stages of Imperialism
    - began to spread after 1870
    - reached its peak between 1880 and 1900
- resulted in a mad scramble for territory by European governments
- was more emotional, nationalistic, and connected to a nation's industry and cultural consciousness than the earlier Imperialism

Rationalism:
- a mechanistic systems of values and view of the universe proposing that:
    - all things could be understood through the application of reason
    - reason alone, unaided by experience, can arrive at basic truth regarding the world
- defined as "any view appealing to reason as a source of knowledge or justification"
- arose at about the same time as modern science
- comparable to deductive reasoning
- best articulated (along with materialism) by René Descartes
- opposes Empiricism (which relies on experience), the theory promoted by John Locke

Romanticism:
- school of thought that emphasizes:
  - feeling and emotion over calculation and rationality
  - the individual
  - irrationalism
- Jean-Jacques Rousseau is seen as the father of Romanticism

Self-Governance:
- began to be desired by Great Britain's colonies, starting with Canada
- by 1914, Australia, New Zealand, and South Africa had also achieved self-government

Socialism:
- an economic system characterized by society as whole owning and controlling the means of production and managing the economy together in a cooperative way
- becomes communism when in its complete form
- the terms socialism and communism were used interchangeably in the 19th century
- modern definition of a socialist:
  - person who believes that collectivization should be accomplished through democratic processes

Surrealism:
- a key artistic movement in which disturbing images were used to portray fantasies, dreams and nightmares
- emphasizes the irrational
- promoted by Salvador Dali

Political, Philosophical, and Scientific Ideas

Theory of Evolution:
- promoted the belief in the survival of the fittest
- first formulated by Charles Darwin
- originally applied to biology, but was quickly adapted to economics, society, and politics
- proposes that:
    - plants and animals all evolved from simple to more complex life forms over a long period of time
    - every species produces many more offspring than can possibly survive, resulting in intense competition among individuals for limited resources
    - survivors whose chance genetic mutations helped them to survive spread their genes to their descendants

Utopian Socialism:
- developed in the early 1800s in response to the terrible living conditions of the poor
- supported the elimination of private property and worker ownership of the means of production
- followed by:
    - Charles Fourier
    - Robert Owen
    - Louis Blanc
    - Flora Tristan

Revolutions and Social Reforms

1572 (France):

- thousands of Huguenots were killed by French Catholics in Paris
  - Huguenots, the French Protestants, were also known as Calvinists
  - they were members of the Protestant Reformed Church of France
  - many of the French nobles who were losing power converted from Catholicism to Protestantism
- the massacre became known as the St. Bartholomew's Day Massacre

The late 1600's (England):

- Oliver Cromwell defeated the forces of King Charles I with the New Model Army, which was:
  - well-disciplined
  - trained in the latest military tactics
  - predominantly composed of extreme Puritans called the Independents
    - the Independents believed they were fighting God's battles
- Charles I was brought to trial, executed and his office abolished
  - a great precedent was set
  - the English people saw that, if they wished, they could change the world around them
- the laboring poor played almost no part in this revolution
- while the revolution didn't change the face of Britain, the real issue at hand was the declining gentry
- Puritans attempted to enforce "Blue Laws", which:
  - prohibited such ordinary pleasures as gambling, horse racing, and theater
  - are still used throughout the world today, though they are gradually being taken off the books

1685 (France):
- Louis XIV revoked the Edict of Nantes (which had guaranteed the Huguenots liberty of worship)
- revocation of the Edict of Nantes attacked the following human rights:
    - full liberty of conscience and private worship
    - liberty of public worship wherever it had previously been granted
    - full civil rights including the right to hold public office
    - royal subsidies for Protestant schools special courts, composed of Roman Catholic and Protestant judges, to judge cases involving Protestants
- the king's goal was to compel the Huguenots to accept Catholicism
- the Huguenots then suffered official persecution
    - dragoons, or soldiers, were housed in Huguenot districts
    - terrible persecutions were inflicted on those who refused to abandon their faith

    - pastors and many others were driven into exile
    - worship was prohibited
- the persecution and resulting exile weakened France, as many workers, soldiers, and officers fled for their lives

1689 (England):
- the Act of Toleration of 1689 finally granted Protestant dissenters in England legal recognition and toleration
- dissenting Protestants were allowed to have their own teachers, preachers, services and churches
- Catholics and those who did not believe in the Trinity were expressly excluded from the benefits of the Act
- Taxpayers hated the tithe levied by the church, even though the full 10 percent was seldom demanded
- Tithe was the French implication of ten percent donation suggested by the church

1700's (Agricultural Revolution):
- enabled farmers to feed more people at lower prices with less labor
- paved the way for the Industrial Revolution by freeing up labor for manufacturing and industrial enterprises
    - rapid population growth in the second half of the eighteenth century provided a pool of surplus labor for the new British factories of the Industrial Revolution
- freed up labor for manufacturing and industrial enterprises

1780— Industrial Revolution:
- many of the technological inventions associated with the Industrial Revolution were actually created before that time
- was enabled or driven by:
    - James Watt's invention of the steam engine in 1769
    - the rapid development of coal mining which resulted from increased demand by iron smelters and for steam power
    - the Railway Age:
        - coal powered railways, and railways transported the coal
        - iron and steel rails made it possible to carry huge weights
        - giant locomotives were invented that could pull long trains
    - profound social as well as technological change
        - the economic revolution in England and the political revolution in France led to very complex patterns of cause and effect
- resulted in:
    - population impact (the largest effect):
        - monumental changes in the structure and distribution of population
            - wherever mines and factories opened, towns and cities appeared
            - large areas that had once been rural now became populated
        - urbanization was accelerated because industry worked most efficiently on the basis of concentrated centers of production

- a population explosion in many societies
  - as some experienced a dramatic rise in the standard of living and others experienced harsh conditions, there was a desire to have greater control over birth and death rates
  - France, where contraceptive methods and abortion in post-revolutionary society led to a decline in birth rates, was the exception to that trend
- social change:
  - increased class consciousness:
    - a growing divide between the middle and working classes
    - a rapidly increasing perception of wealth inequality between the rich and poor
    - fostered by the concentration of workers in metropolitan areas
    - pauperism was most visible in the cities
  - poor working conditions
    - excessively long hours
    - low pay
    - rigorous discipline
    - dehumanizing working conditions
    - hazardous work with a lack of safety devices to guard dangerous machinery
  - many opportunities for women to work in factories
    - women were still paid less than men for performing the same job, as they have been throughout history
  - child labor:
    - by the 1820s, employment of children in textiles and mining had become a disgrace in England
    - stories of child labor cruelty inflamed public opinion in the 1820s and 1830s
    - children on their hands and knees, pulling carts of coal through mine shafts for years on end

- the Factory Act of 1833:
  - forbade employment of children under 9 years of age
  - limited the number of hours children under 13 could work
- the transformation of European society from an rural agricultural society into a capitalist, urban, and industrial society by the year 1890
  - Russia was one of the last countries to experience the Industrial Revolution
- new tastes in art, literature, and music
- many people in industrial nations remained semi-literate
- free education finally became widely available in the late 1800s
- economic transformation:
  - prolonged inflation from 1848 to 1873
  - a long period of English prosperity after the 1760's
  - the consolidation of labor in large factories, creating economies of scale
  - smaller profit margins which made it difficult if not impossible for smaller businesses to compete
  - transformation of textile manufacturing from a largely cottage-based practice to a mechanized industry which allowed the production of vast quantities of fabric, allowing exportation on a grand scale
    - dominated by Spain
  - focused on the creation of national trade unions in the 1820s and 1830s
  - union movements to protect worker rights
    - the creation of national trade unions in the 1820s and 1830s
  - development of a global economy
  - an improvement in the British standard of living, though not until after the Napoleonic Wars and postwar slump were over
  - an increase in purchasing power for workers as more and cheaper goods became available

- purchasing power of the workers seems to have grown very gradually, starting in 1820
  - banks encouraged economic expansion by promoting the use of checks and bank notes in place of coins
  - this change resulted from economic conditions during the Napoleonic wars, when a shortage of coins forced some British mill owners to pay their workers in goods, leading the British government to empower local banks to issue paper notes to supplementing the meager supply of coins
- faster communication
  - The Penny Post started in England in 1840
    - a letter could go from London to Edinburgh for one penny
    - this was less than a tenth of the old rate
- health challenges
  - disease epidemics triggered by unsanitary working conditions
    - urban reformers advocated sanitary reforms such as efficient sewer systems and clean water
    - due to their fear of cholera, many middle class citizens supported public health reforms
- development of commercial and public transportation
  - the first railway for public transportation opened in Liverpool, England in 1830
    - featuring a steam-powered locomotive, it ran 32 miles from Liverpool to Manchester
    - prior to this, rail cars were used only in mining and were pulled by horses
    - travelers soon began speaking of distances traveled in terms of time rather than miles

- while railway systems improved travel for people, they also enabled more efficient trading of goods

1800's (England):
- England emerges as a parliamentary democracy in which the cabinet controlled Parliament
- representation was increased through the extension of suffrage and the reform of electoral districts
- the corn laws were repealed
  - in England the word corn referred to all different grains

1775-1783 (American Revolution):
- war for independence from English control, fought by the 13 United States colonies

1787-1788 (France):
- bad harvests and a manufacturing depression caused food shortages, high inflation, and skyrocketing unemployment
- due to costly wars and massive spending on royal projects, the French government didn't have any money saved up for a crisis
- King Louis XVI desperately tried to avoid bankruptcy and at last reluctantly summoned the Estates General

1789 (France—the French Revolution):
- preceded by a financial crisis—like most revolutions
  - the near collapse of French government finances is viewed as the cause
- directly connected to the American revolution of 1776 (Revolutionary War)
- resulted in:
  - political, social, and religious upheaval
  - major changes to the government and clergy based on Enlightenment principles
  - mounting criticism of the clergy and their role in the "Old Regime"
  - the emergence and evolution of the "New Regime"

Revolutions and Social Reforms

1830 (across Europe):
- revolutions occurred across Europe during this year
- the primary cause of the revolutions were liberalism and nationalism.
- the biggest areas of revolution were France, Belgium, Poland, and the Italian states

1830 (Belgium):
- Belgium won independence from the Dutch in a revolution known as the Belgium Revolt
- a constitutional monarchy was established

1830's (England):
- Britain's ruling party, the Whigs, recognized that:
  - the demands of the middle class could no longer be ignored
  - it was better to make some early concessions than to suffer a revolution later
- as a result, they had passed considerable reform legislation
- England was peaceful during the 1830's because of those liberal reforms

1830 (Germany):
- The "Young Germans, consisting of a group of young authors, organize
- their movement resulted from the July, 1830 revolution in Paris
- The "Young Germans":
  - they advocated political action in order to achieve republican ideals
  - had a supporter named Heinrich Heine

1832 (England):
- Reform Bill of 1832 accomplished revolutionary changes in England without violence
- was favorable to the British industries and economy

1848 (across Europe):
- revolutions occurred across Europe during this year
- the primary cause of the revolutions were liberalism and nationalism.
- the biggest areas of revolution were France, Belgium, Poland, and the Italian states
- Russia and England were about the only nations in Europe to avoid a revolution during this year
- Russia avoided the revolution because of brutal repression
  - failure to adjust to the times & attempts to preserve the autocratic rule produced discontent in Russia

1848 (England):
- witnessed revolutions in most of Europe but ended without a major crisis in England
- England and Russia were about the only two nations in Europe to escape a revolution during this year

1848 (Germany):
- popular uprising led to the dismissal of unpopular ministers
- occurred when the people wanted a national parliament to draft a constitution for a united Germany
- failed because 3 kinds of problems—economic, liberal, and national, were not easily fixed

1850 (England):
- England began to lose its advantage in the economic community

1850's (Russia):
- angry Russian citizens finally forced through the changes they had wanted since the 1930's and 1940's

1867 (England):
- Reform Bill of 1867 accomplished revolutionary changes in England without violence

Revolutions and Social Reforms

1871 (France):
- The Paris Commune, a short-lived government, takes over Paris after the Franco-Prussian War
- was in opposition to the national government which controlled the rest of France
- a large part of the populace was actively involved in public affairs
- the members of the Commune were delegates of the people, not parliamentary members
- lasted only a few months before national government troops entered Paris and regained control of the city

Early 1900's:
- saw the rise in popularity of eugenics, a bio-social movement aimed at "improving the genetics" of a population
- widely popular in the early 1900's
- interest in spurred by enthusiasm for "racial purity"
- led to widespread athleticism and a cult of physical health

1918-1921:
- the first period of post-Revolution Soviet history
- dominated by militant communism and military events
- "War Communism" or "Military Communism" was the political system in place during that period
- all parties within the Russian Government except a small group within the Social Democratic Party supported entry into World War I
    - Russian government received much aid in the war effort from voluntary committees, including representatives of business and labor
    - the growing breakdown of supply, made worse by the almost complete isolation of Russia from its prewar markets, was felt especially in the major cities, which were flooded with refugees from the front
    - many Duma leaders felt that Russia would soon be confronted with a new revolutionary crisis

Post World War I (1919-1939):
- marked by political movements to the right in various countries
- featured some commonalities between the conservative movements, although they were in different cultures
- Britain, France, and the U.S. were preoccupied with domestic problems
- the urgent financial crisis of the Great Depression during the early 1930's increased this preoccupation
- uncertainty pervaded the cultural and intellectual achievements of artists and writers
- pre-war beliefs suggesting that human beings were violent and irrational creatures, completely incapable of creating a sane and rational world, were seen as validated by the horrors or World War I

The Great Depression (approximately 1929—1940):
- a severe worldwide economic depression
- triggered by the Stock Market Crash of 1929
    - U. S. stock market crash credited to the uneven prosperity of the Coolidge years and unprecedented speculation on Wall Street
- unprecedented in its length and in the wholesale poverty and tragedy inflicted on society
- seen as resulting from war debts and reparations
- eased by a one year moratorium on intergovernmental debts, championed by Herbert Hoover in 1931

Cold War (1947-1991):
- Two military superpowers emerged—the United States and the Soviet Union
- The Soviets used the war to expand their empire, imposing totalitarian governments throughout the territories they occupied as a result of the war
- Western democracies briefly occupied conquered nations, but gradually allowed them to return to self-rule

1960's—1970's:
- in the 1960s and 1970s, European women worked to repeal laws which had outlawed birth control and abortion
- even Catholic countries passed legislation permitting abortion and contraception by the 1980s

1973:
- the Oil Crisis brought the "golden sixties" to an end
- devastated the economies of Western industrialized nations
- resulted in a serious drop in real income in 1975 (the first reduction since 1958) and a dramatic increase in inflation

Made in the USA
Middletown, DE
26 January 2020